Grow The ----- Up!
You Fill In The Blank!

Grow The ----- Up!
You Fill In The Blank!

A Guide for Living dedicated to
Changing YOURSELF to ensure you
live the rest of your life Drama-Free!

MARGO NORMAN

iUniverse, Inc.
Bloomington

Grow The ------ Up! You Fill In The Blank!
A Guide for Living dedicated to Changing YOURSELF to ensure you live the rest of your life Drama-Free!

iUniverse books may be ordered through booksellers or by contacting:

iUniverse
1663 Liberty Drive
Bloomington, IN 47403
www.iuniverse.com
1-800-Authors (1-800-288-4677)

ISBN: 978-1-4759-6478-3 (sc)
ISBN: 978-1-4759-6479-0 (ebk)

Library of Congress Control Number: 2012922732

Printed in the United States of America

iUniverse rev. date: 11/29/2012

Contents

I Am More Than Qualified!

After 40 years of living this life, I found that people ask me for my opinion and advice often. I figured that qualifies me to offer some MUCH Needed thoughts from my very ample store of advice, and if you find your situation addressed in this book, (which you probably will); then KNOW that I've gone through that same situation. I wrote this book for all of my sisters, *"sistahs"*, and females over the age of 18, because; to be truthful, it seems as though you are suffering with "SPDS—Self-Perpetuated Drama Syndrome"! Not all of you, but a large amount of you ladies.

It came as a shock that I would be the one the "message" came through, but I am a firm believer that GOD in HIS infinite wisdom has a plan and a process in place for you to carry out your **PURPOSE** in this life! So, ladies read on, and find the truths in the situations that are touched on in this book. Be assured that although some of these circumstances can be humorous, that this is **SERIOUS** advice. I have been known to suffer with S.P.D.S. more than once in a while. It wasn't until a life altering situation happened to affect my daily living that I came to realize exactly how much of my own drama was my own fault.

I now know better, and after twenty-four years of relentless drama, I decided to use my experiences to try to help others. GOD showed me what HE created me for and now I utilize my skills to glorify HIM who blessed me with these skills to begin with. So get out the Kleenex, the French Vanilla Coffee, and tell the kids that Mommy needs some personal time, because the journey to living a drama-free life started when you picked this book to read, and the trip; although short, is riddled with deep self-evaluations and hard decisions.

Some will make you laugh, some may make you cry; but all of them are supposed to be used as learning tools to help cure your SPDS. You may have the need for the Kleenex. The coffee is to help us stay focused—remember we are trying to change for the better. I also advise that you get a notebook to help you keep track of what you have learned so far and to reflect on certain things that catch your eye. You can write them down so as not to forget them. Then when you're done reading, you can use the notebook to gather more information, or advice from others, for feedback, or whatever you want to write down. Now ladies, let's begin.

This book is ten chapters long, with a few sub-chapters. Each chapter is dedicated to a different topic, but all of them coincide with each other. Everyone who reads this book to try to help cure their SPDS might be interested in one of these topics or all of them. I recommend reading the whole book, so you may benefit the most from the advice being given. Remember, these are ***my personal*** opinions and thoughts, not a "*BIG WORDS*" situation.

You have the right to "***love it or lump it***" as the saying goes. I ***am NOT*** singling anyone out (*my friends and family). I am talking about things and situations that we have all experienced. So please no phone calls, texts or unnecessary arguments because you feel that I am speaking about any one person directly. I speak about that in "Chapter 3: Sometimes It's NOT About YOU!"

Enjoy and I pray that you benefit somehow by reading my book.

Chapter 1: Grow the _____ Up!

The first time I said I was writing a book addressing certain issues pertaining to "AGE-APPROPRIATE BEHAVIOR"; I was greatly encouraged by my family and friends. I received a lot of "girl, it's about time!" and "took you long enough", and even one "I've been waiting". My friends more so than my family, had a lot of advice **FOR ME** on what I should or shouldn't expound upon. My favorite comments were the ones that came from the very people that need this advice **MORE** than everyone else.

YOU KNOW THIS FRIEND! You have one too. She or He says "you should write about such and such and so and so!" Well, I decided to write about everyone that suffers with S.P.D. Syndrome. The symptoms of SPDS are very recognizable. The first, and most often; worst symptom is known as "age-inappropriate behavior". This is very common in today's women.

Age-appropriate behavior is "acting in a manner consistent with one's age". So a lot of women have a problem with this topic. After having researched this subject extensively; I came to the conclusion that we; (women) are constantly lying about how old we are to fight being viewed as "old". I did a poll of 150 women, over the age of 18 and the two questions I asked were followed by more than a few extremely immature responses. The first question was "how old are you?", and the second was "how old do you **behave**"? What follows are a few of these answers.

Question 1: HOW OLD ARE YOU?

Now I found myself asking women in New York City (where I live) this particular question at least twice, because the first answer generally was a lie. For example; "Sheila D." from Brooklyn was asked twice because she had a birthday coming up (her 21ˢᵗ) and she was lying "up", so she could buy liquor legally before her birthday officially arrived, while "Erma W." from Queens was lying "down" so she could find a younger guy. Erma is fifty-four, looks forty, and that's what she told me the first time I asked her age.

This practice of lying about your age is considered the "norm" in our American society. I just recently turned forty, and up until last year; I was telling people I was twenty-five! So, I'm not immune to SPDS because I truly didn't realize that people treat you the way you *allow* them too, based on **How YOU TREAT YOURSELF**! If you say you're twenty-five, then; you'll be treated like you're twenty-five. Get It?

Question 2: How old do you behave?

Age appropriate behavior reflects the general behavior associated with any particular age. Like a five year old is generally known for being curious about *everything*, while a 28 year old is known to be questioning the future of their aging process. If a 5 year old was asking "should I wear the pink thong or the blue thong panties", you would immediately say to the child; "neither—you're too young for thongs" and probably fuss at the parent of said child. If a 28 year old was asked what her favorite T.V. show is, and her response is **ANYTHING** on one of the kid-specific cable stations; you would immediately shake your head and try to give her a "Maturity Lecture"! That said, let's take a look at the answers given by our two women, Sheila D. and Erma W.* (not their real names) that I chose to emphasize on.

Sheila's response to how old she behaves was really no surprise to me because I had a fake I.D. made when I was eighteen and trying to get into the dance clubs with my older friends. Amazingly enough, her answer totally matched the actions of a twenty year old. She said she behaved like a "Grown-up", because she has her own apartment and she pays her own bills and takes care of her four children ALL By Herself! Now I know that being twenty isn't equated with most peoples definition of being "grown-up", but let's examine why this young woman, and others about her age feel that they are "grown".

Most adult females feel that they're grown because they were taught how to be an adult while still living at home with their parents *(discussed in chp.5-You're grown so buy your own!). We are taught as little girls to take care of ourselves physically, encouraged to be independent, and to care for others. This is to ensure self-reliance when we reach adulthood. Some of us have strayed from what we were taught and we made certain choices that sped up the growing process. These choices turned out badly and we began to fall back on what "my Momma taught me", thereby stunting our spiritual growth as well as our ability to think for ourselves in a positive, mature way.

Now please don't misunderstand. I am not saying your mother was wrong for teaching independence. I'm saying she should have allowed you to be a child first, then; as you grew older and needed to learn "womanly things", she should have taught you how to navigate young adulthood with a bit more care and discretion. When a twenty-year-old mother of four can proudly announce to the world that she's "grown", I believe she should **KNOW** that being an "grown" is about more than "paying my own bills" and "I don't have to ask anybody for anything".

She should have been taught about birth control, and about making healthy choices with her life and for the lives of her children. Instead she was taught "YOU ARE OUT OF MY HOUSE THE MINUTE YOU TURN 18! You're legally able to vote and buy your own cigarettes, you're GROWN"! *HOW SO VERY WRONG THIS IS*! Now this young lady is taught to believe that she is "grown" because she can pay a bill, but emotionally and mentally will remain a child herself. Did you ever meet a "grown-up" that was younger than forty? Heck, I know women in their fifties who make me question their mental age.

Now we reintroduce Erma W. again, because of that very question. When asked how old she behaved, she immediately had a negative response: "so . . . exactly what is it that you are trying to say? That I'm immature or something?" Now that immediate response caused Erma to be viewed as immature and not capable of holding an intelligent conversation for more than two minutes. I might also add that her physical appearance left a lot to be desired in the age-appropriately behaved category, but we'll discuss that later. Did I also mention that Erma is Caucasian? SPDS like AIDS; does not discriminate!

My poll showed that of those 150 women, 50 were over fifty but looked younger, fifty were younger than thirty, but looked older, and fifty looked their age and more importantly, were behaving age appropriately. (Incidentally, those last fifty women were over forty). Now the purpose of this little survey was to prove to myself that I wasn't imagining the amount of DRAMA I see EVERY SINGLE DAY, perpetuated by so-called "grown-assed women".

I decided to do something that I pray helps some of you "G.A.W."s. I grew the ____up and wrote this book, because there are a lot more Sheila's and Erma's out there! There are Beth's, Patty's and Sally's and Shaniqua's, Taisha's and Laquita's, as well. There are definitely Margo's. Ok, I'm playing about the other Margo's, but you get the idea, especially if you truly are an adult woman. You'll know you're *GROWN* when you can admit that ***YOU'RE NOT GROWN***!

Don't worry though. I'm going to attempt to help you "***grow the ____up***" and learn how to become a woman who doesn't have to lie about her age. I'll start with me. I am forty and I behave like I'm a woman that takes her age seriously because with age comes wisdom and with wisdom, comes responsibility: in other words; I am forty and I'm a woman about my forty year old business. Now, if you'd please join me in chapter 2.

[A quick thought: Who did you see in your mind when you saw Sheila and Erma's responses to my two questions? Write the names of these two women in your note book and write each of them a letter explaining that they should buy this book. If you saw yourself in either Sheila or Erma, you have obviously figured out that you're not grown; though you may be an adult because you've already grown up mentality and figured out that you have a problem.]

CHAPTER 2 : WHAT THE * * * ARE YOU WEARING?!?

Ladies, please see this next situation as clearly as possible, because we have all had it happen at least once in our lives; more than once in my case. Like every time I venture into the public eye (which is not often anymore.) You are out, taking care of business; its 9 or 10 o'clock in the morning. You're in a rush to get your agenda followed, so you're really not noticing the people around you. Then "She" walks by. You know her or someone like her. She's got to be over thirty, yet you really can't tell because of the way she's dressed.

She has on a leopard print mini skirt in a broad spectrum of neon colors: pink and green and orange, and wait up, is that yellow and gold sparkles on this monstrosity of a swatch of material so short that it looks like a tube top that she squeezed her size 28 hips into? She has on 6 inch stiletto's, open toes and her feet are not done and sticking out over the top of the shoes. She is definitely told old for the bang of hot pink, synthetic hair sitting on her forehead, framing the extremely colorful make-up on her face. She's loud and hasn't spoken a word. Her outrageous appearance has said it all for her.

You are amazed! What the heck was she thinking when she got dressed this morning? Was she thinking at all? You just shake your head like it's a shame, and keep on about your business. Then, you reach your destination; and, lo and behold; here "She" comes. She chooses to be next to you and you turn your head because you don't want anyone to think you're together, or worse; that you may be related!!! So, you finish your business and get as far away from her as you physically can.

The minute you get home or to the office, or around other people, you tell anyone that's willing to listen about "her". Her state of dress has left you feeling nothing but animosity at her. You're thinking out loud to yourself "I would *NEVER* be seen in public dressed **like THAT**"!! You vow that you will never get caught up in the "being too old to wear that" mode. Am I correct? Of course I am.

I don't speak from what I heard; I speak from what I KNOW, through self—experience. You see, I have BEEN "her" on more than one occasion throughout my forty years. At each age (once I was allowed to buy my own clothes), I had at least one "real shocker" of an outfit. I'll tell you about a few. There was the off-the—shoulder, neon green, spandex mini-skirt at the age of twenty. How about my tiger print, black and hot pink lace bustier, black booty shorts; with hot pink, patent leather, 6 inch stiletto thigh high boots? I was twenty-five.

I can't forget my favorite "Her" outfit of all time: an electric blue and hot pink track suit, with the word "***BOOTY-LISCIOUS***" written across the behind, in gold letters with blue and pink highlights. Worst yet; I had on matching high-heel sneakers and a fitted baseball cap. Let me tell you truthfully, I looked "A HOT MESS!!" I even matched my accessories! I was thirty. I learned how to dress age-appropriate one night, when my girlfriends and I went to a dance club, and I wore that last outfit. I got to the club, and the skinny chick that was my "club twin" looked better than me in the same outfit. She was 21, and weighed 125 pounds, soaking wet and holding a brick!

Now; let me describe myself a little more. I am 5 ft., 4 in. tall and weigh 223 lbs. I am forty now, and I learned to dress age-appropriately, because when you're a size 18-20 for a few years, you can't wear certain kinds of clothes anymore. When you're "grown", you recognize that "showing-off" is really no longer necessary. You realize that; no matter what you're wearing, YOU ARE COMFORTABLE! "She" is NOT COMFORTABLE! We'll go there in another chapter. The point is, I grew the ___up and learned some things and now I can share what I've learned with others.

I learned to match my mental age to my physical one. I learned to choose more age-appropriate clothing. I stopped picking up the shortest, tightest thing and realized that I DIDN'T LOOK GOOD! Or should I say "ADMITTED TO MY SELF"? I realized that I needed a quick self—evaluation. My "back-tits", my "front-booty", my "love-muffins", my "jellyrolls", my "cookies", hell; the whole damned bakery needed renovation! When I say I was a hot mess fashion-wise, honey; I mean it! We all have had a moment in our fashion history when we bought the REAL SHOCKER!

I bet you were so uncomfortable that you had at least one part of that outfit OFF before you reached home! Honey even now; if something is pinching, pulling, rising up, or falling down; it's out of there! I spent the better part of my twenties and thirties dressing inappropriately. I was always angry because I was uncomfortable WITH and IN these apparent cries for help. My self-esteem borders on egotism. I didn't need the "EXTRA" look, but it was my CHOICE and I thought I was "grown" (there goes that word again). I made some horrible fashion decisions.

I can look back now and see how much I've grown up, because today when I go out, I am confident that I don't look like "HER", and WON'T ever AGAIN!

Women; regardless of race, geographic location, or financial status like to look good. You can relate. If you have to wear coverings like other countries, you still try to get the prettiest material to wear. EVEN Better, your shoes cost a lot more than "hers" because that's all anyone can see. I know. I practiced Islam at one time, (I really was that much in need of GOD), so again; I'm speaking from what I know.

I pray that all you "She's" out there are getting what I am trying to tell them. Dressing appropriately stops a lot of unnecessary SPDS from going on. If you're angry at yourself because your shoes are pinching your toes and your tights are sliding down because they're too damned small or your PHONY-tail is too tight and the bobby pins are sticking you in the middle of your head, you will eventually learn to dress age-appropriate. You'll learn, that when you're comfortably dressed; you're nicer to people (that's because you can breathe and you're less likely to be in a bad mood if you're not in pain).

Now I have listed a few DO's and Don'ts for you ladies (especially you plus-sized Sweeties), in terms of being age-appropriately dressed for every situation where your fashion sense directly affects your behavior. I started with "the Job Interview". This is specifically because I have seen some "real shockers" at such an event. Let me start by saying that the words "job interview" does not bring the "hooker gone good" look to mind, unless; of course you are applying for a job as a waitress at "MILO's House of Beer and Broads—*where the only things that wear a top is the beer*!".

DO's:

DO—Eat BEFORE you go shopping! People tend to think much clearer on a full stomach. Therefore your choices will reflect your relaxed state of mind. The clothes you buy will fit you just right because your full stomach will shrink back down later. If it fits too snug when you try it on, you'll be more apt to get the next size up. Also, you will know that you can eat a meal in it and not be uncomfortable.

DO—BUY YOUR CORRECT SIZE! I cannot stress this point enough! No-one else wants to see that your "bakery" is "overstocked"! You might think that skinny jeans, tank tops and 6 inch stilettoes on a 5 ft., 4 inch, over 220 pound frame is "sexy"; but I promise you, it's **NOT**! Now some of my "Big Girls" are going to be mad at me; but truth will prevail in an instant if you're **honest** with yourself. At no time should you be even considering purchasing a "skinny" anything!

YOU ARE NOT SKINNY, so why would you choose those size 18 jeans when you're a 22? And any shirt or blouse that clearly doesn't offer coverage of your "chicken wings" is also not considered reasonable. If I am an employer, I am not only reading and discussing your resume', I am also giving your attire scrutiny because if you could not pick out a decent—fitting outfit for the interview, how am I supposed to believe that you'll be an asset to my company? You're going to need good decision making capabilities, and your attire shows what kind of choices you make in your personal life. So ladies, always wear your size.

DO—Invest in a quality "self-investment" suit. A self-investment suit is the dress and jacket or the skirt/slacks and jacket that is a direct reflection of your comfort in your fashion choices, the suit of clothes that you would wear to a specified event. It shows your commitment to being appropriately dressed hence; you will behave like you're confident in your abilities, instead of sitting through the interview fidgeting because your panty—hose are too small.

DO—Make sure that your hemlines and cleavage are not too revealing. Again I cannot stress this point enough. Even plus sized princesses look better when there is a bit of mystery about them. Really ladies, NO-ONE wants to see your double-D's out for the whole world to view. Your breast are already large, you don't need to show them off any more than is necessary.

DO—Invest In A GOOD BRA! If you are a plus-sized sweetie, let me be perfectly clear on this point. You are abundantly blessed with an ample bosom. You definitely need proper support for those torpedoes. The fashion magazines tell you to go bra shopping at least 2-3 times a year because of weight gain or loss, so you really should be measured to avoid "back tits" and puckering. If your bra straps are cutting into your shoulder or your bands are twisting and pinching, then the bra is too small.

Get measured, then, purchase bras in your size. Also; know exactly which styles suit your cup size. I don't expect to see DD's in a midi-cup, or an underwire demi-cup. If you want "sexy", shop at a plus-size specific lingerie store. Ask the clerk for something that suits your taste, budget and style.

DO—Choose clothes in prints, patterns, and colors that reflect not only your personal style, but also states that you're confident in your self-view. Play to your positive strengths. If you weigh over 200 pounds, unless you're going to a party, ***ANY sheer material is NOT RECCOMMENDED*** (bold colors either)! Where are you going, with the neon green and gold, metallic, sequined mini dress; that is showing your cellulite and stretch marks? Are you *really serious*? You have that much confidence, which is excellent, but is it really necessary to prove this by looking like you shopped at "HO's R US"?

What's up with the busted feet hanging over the tops of those little—assed, high, thin heeled shoes? You're supposed to be at a job interview, attending to "grown woman" business.

I have a story that is perfect for this situation. If you're familiar with West Indian culture, then you know that after a funeral, there is generally a party to celebrate the deceased person's life. Most people call it the repast. A few years ago, a good friend's father passed away. At the repast, my friend's aunt told a story for the sake of the inappropriately dressed cousins in attendance. She said that while she was shopping for her funeral outfit, she saw her "She".

The aunt said; "As I was coming out of the shoe store, there she was; bold as you please! She had to be at least 250 lbs. She had on this little skirt, and all of her breast exposed; but the problem was her shoes. Impossible shoes, the heel was so long and skinny, I don't know how she could walk in them. I mean, from what I could see, she couldn't even stand up on those heels. I stopped to watch her for a minute because I just knew those heels were going to break and I waited to see if she would break a bone when her big behind fell. It took her ten minutes to walk from one store entrance to the next, and every time she took a step; she dipped and she wobbled, she dipped and she shook. She looked crazy!!"

I tell that story for two reasons. The first is because I have always worn heels, and times when I "just had to *HAVE*" that pair of little, strappy stilettos. Once I gained the weight that makes skinny heels *NOT* an option, I have broken the heels of at least 3 pairs of really expensive shoes. The other reason is because I know better than to wear "***Impossible Shoes***" to begin with! The doctors all over the world tell us that heels aren't good for our feet any way. So a plus-sized girl should be doing anything ***but*** wearing shoes that offer no stability, no support for the hips, back and thighs. If you are wearing "impossible shoes" and you are a "BIG GIRL"; over the age of 18, you should take this to heart!

DO—Buy a nice 2-3 inch wedge or pump heeled shoe in the next half size up from your size! If you wear a size 8 shoe, by all means buy an 8 ½ or 9 (for heels, because your feet will slide)! Oh yeah; one more thing: GET THOSE FEET DONE!! I know a lot of you feel this! How are you going anywhere with your feet looking like you just walked through a mine field bare foot? So now; you have ashy heels *AND* your toes are sticking over the tops of the shoes and dragging the ground! Girlfriend all I can say is "REALLY"?

Now, we've covered age-appropriate behavior through our style of dress. The next few things are after thoughts.

Please be aware that perfume is an Accessory, like a hat, shoes and jewelry. You only need a light misting—(spray it up in the air and walk under it so that it lands evenly over you). Ladies also; jewelry should be kept to a minimum. Where is your "grown" ass going with twenty bracelets going up your arm or three or more chains hanging around your neck?

If you have tattoos and/or piercings, I would like to remind you that when in public, whatever you display is your ***CHOICE***! At thirty years of age, I got my tongue pierced. I had my own reasons for having it done, but I knew better than to tell my mom I had it. She would have passed away without knowing I had a piercing because I didn't display it for her (or anyone else except my husband to be. DON'T FRONT, you know what a tongue ring is for)! One of my big mouth relations let her see his and the next thing I know; I'm being smacked on the back of my head because I wasn't supposed to get anything on my body "poked through or anything written on it either!"

Unless you're somewhere that your tats and piercings are accepted, cover them up!

One last thing: A lot of people feel that the wearing of big flower rings, bright neon colors (on your body and/or hair), animal and flower prints (***especially ANIMAL PRINTS AND FLOWER PRINTS!!);*** should be illegal for plus-sized princesses! Why? Do you really feel comfortable in the leopard or zebra, looking like the ENTIRE ZOO? Do you believe you look anything other than a HOT AND STINKING MESS?!? A Tiger is sleek, svelte, and sexy. You are ***NOT*** an animal, why would you want to dress like one? GOD, in HIS infinite wisdom; gave these animals beautiful designs and colors, but HE put neon colors on the flowers and plants, **NOT ON YOU**! (*Or the lions and tigers, and bears either.* Oh My)!

GOD gave you a creative will, to show your creativity and all you could come up with is an electric blue and black, zebra—striped, mini dress? What blue leopard do you see in fifteen bangles, 4 rings on each paw, 5 earrings in its face and ears, and smelling like it took a bath in some cheap cologne? I'm shaking my head, because never once in forty years have I seen this outfit on an animal. What the damned shame about this situation *is NOT* your inappropriate attire, but; the *attitudes* that portray you as an animal when these outrageous outfits are being worn! (See: ERMA W.—Chapter 1)

The point of all this is to advise you to think more carefully about the choices that you in make in your life. People; even though THE BIBLE tells us not to judge, we do so anyway. I described the woman with the "dip and wobble" to see where your head went. If you immediately thought of another person, you're standing in judgment of her. (I discuss this in another chapter.)

I say these things to assure you that you're not alone. I say this to let my sisters, "*sistahs*", and all of you women know that in order to stop suffering with SPDS, you must first achieve the mindset of a "grown woman"! Please don't feel like I am judging you. I am simply trying to give you some REAL advice. I want to help you be the YOU that GOD made you to be! You are not "HER", and even if you *were* "HER" before you read this; **YOU'RE NOT "HER" NOW!**

CHAPTER 3: SOME TIMES, IT'S NOT ABOUT YOU!!

Well, Actually IT IS ABOUT YOU!!!

I turned forty a few months ago, and I was a little confused on what that was supposed to represent in my life. I found myself loathing the fast-approaching truth that I am a "GROWN-ASSED WOMAN"! I needed to find out over the last four decades exactly what GOD wanted from and FOR me. What was revealed to me was this book. I am supposed to have learned from my life exactly what I can and cannot do and to help others from following my very bad example; starting with my own daughters and sons.

I now see why I had SO MUCH DRAMA in my life. GOD, in HIS infinite wisdom; was showing me **WHO** was responsible for the drama. HE pulled me through so much nonsense! I'm thankful to HIM and HIM alone for saving me from **MYSELF**. Now that *who* was causing this drama has been revealed to me, I took off my "blinders" and in the words of one of my favorite rappers (TRINA); I matched my panties and my bra and got my Shit together! This book is proof of that.

I've led quite the eventful life, always busy; never boring. It also wasn't peaceful, and just recently became "fruitful". I had a lot to learn about being considered "grown". I had to learn how to have age-appropriate become a major part of my life. Now, I will tell you about the defining moment. Let me tell you though; I was scared that no-one would listen to me, that no-one needed my advice. I found out that I was wrong and my faith wasn't as strong as I had been "PRETENDING" it was.

My life altering situation I spoke about earlier was the death of my mother 3 years ago. Her death was followed within four months by the birth of my first grandson, (he is beautiful, by the way) and the disaster that IS the relationship my then 17 year old daughter can't seem to pull away from. There was so much drama and I couldn't deal with it. I became clinically depressed and began to internalize every bit of the drama and blame myself. My mind wouldn't allow me to be involved in my daughter's life in a progressive way. I felt like a "bad person" because of my daughter's choices to live a life filled with SPDS. ***THIS IS WHY I KNOW I WASN'T GROWN***!!

Since I have always had negative responses to potentially stressful situations, I have always internalized other people's problems and take non-beneficial actions when faced with stress. Here's an example: when I was about 28, I had to get a certain document from our Bureau of Vital Statistics. If you live in a city with a large population, you can relate to my frustration because I had to stand on the line for almost three hours, from around 9 o'clock am until almost 12pm.I was slightly aggravated, a little hungry and a lot dizzy. When the extremely large man standing behind me on the line made a comment about people coming into government agencies drunk before noon; I jumped to the wrong conclusion and responded.

It turns out that he thought I was drunk because I had been weaving for at least a half hour. The air conditioner was broken and you know a lot of people gathered in any kind of small space create heat. I was very rude to that man. I said if he didn't like drunks in government agencies, then maybe he shouldn't get drunk and go into government agencies.

Needless to say; there was an angry exchange of words. It just so happens that I was having a diabetic reaction and since I hadn't been to the doctor since my youngest son was born four years before, I didn't even know I had Diabetes! Growing older and gaining useful knowledge has shown me that I didn't have to respond to him in the first place. It has also shown me that I wasn't acting age-appropriate, because by the time I was twenty-eight; I should have known I was a Diabetic, been treated and taught how to function correctly. I should have been "about grown woman's" business.

I had let my health insurance lapse four years before as well. I was not behaving in sync with my age because at age twenty-eight, I should have had my medical insurance in place and been seen by a medical doctor, a gynecologist, a chiropractor, a dentist, a podiatrist, an optometrist, and any other doctor I may have had a use for, *not excluding a mental health professional*! I didn't because I was busy being "grown". I wasted two decades behaving in-appropriately. I had to learn how to behave as an adult, in every situation—good and bad, that happened in my life. I have learned and let me tell you now; this is where the self-evaluation started.

I had to look into myself for why I was always caught up in some silly stuff. I learned a lot about myself that I didn't approve of. Then last year it was put into perspective for me when my doctor told me that I was diabetic, had high blood pressure, and arthritis in both legs and gouty arthritis in my right foot! She also told me that if I didn't start changing my habits (not only the physical ones like my cigarette smoking and wearing inappropriate shoes), that I wouldn't live to see my fortieth birthday, or the end of last year for that matter! It shook me up pretty badly. So up until last year; I behaved inappropriately for my age.

I wasn't acting like I was thirty-nine, wasn't doing what a "grown" woman of thirty-nine years of age does at all! Worst yet; I was someone's grandmother! I had to grow up quick! I had to learn to take my physical health very seriously. I also had to learn *to NOT* have a response for everything someone says or does to me. I had to learn to **shut-up sometimes**, that silence is the best response to ignorance. I had to leave childish things alone! Talking "smack" is a very childish thing.

As the years have gone by, I have started sorting through what was wrong with my drama filled life. My S.P.D.S. has shown itself so much that I felt like I was wrapped up in it, like I was suffocating in the needless drama, refusing to take advice from others as well as constantly saying "I'm grown"! You can imagine my shock when I discovered that even though I was thirty-nine, and someone's grandmother, and someone's wife-to-be, and a community leader, I was not acting like a grown up; period! Like I said in chapter 2, being grown is about more than being able to pay bills, and single-handedly raising four kids (at twenty years of age), or having my own apartment. This is where my "self-evaluation" came in to play.

As I started digging into my stressful past to get to the root of my daily drama, I discovered that a lot of the stress and mini-dramas could have been avoided *if I*

had just held my tongue! It also showed me that being "grown" meant knowing when and HOW to respond to potentially stressful situations. In other words, **knowing when to talk, how to talk, where to talk, and WHO to talk to**! Let's see if we can be "honest" with ourselves for a moment. Learning to **NOT** respond is the hardest part of growing up.

I will show you a few things that I figured out about my SPDS, the things that taught me how to stop, think and breathe before making potentially dramatic situations worse.

If you know that you've had a hard day at work, or a "bad day"; then going into the supermarket at 6pm, (the most crowed time in most retail businesses), spending two hours shopping and another hour at the checkout line, then cursing out the woman with the three tired, cranky kids on the line in front of you can only be viewed as your own willingness to incite some kind of confrontation, especially if you are over thirty years old. This is not behaving in a manner that is consistent with being thirty plus. If this is what you do regularly, well; you're going to get what you asked for: drama!

At thirty, you tend to wonder if you are truly living up to your potential. At this age, you really shouldn't be engaging in self-perpetuated drama. At this age, going into a bank on payday, during your lunch hour should not turn into you cursing out "that bitch behind the teller's window" because she has to count your money out three times and *she's* making you late to go back to work. Nor should you be caught outside at any time **pushing strangers** out of your way because **you** should have been to your appointment with the exclusive nail technician 10 minutes ago, but that "**heifer**" at the fast-food place didn't put napkins in **your** bag and **you** had to go back.

I had to learn to think before I spoke, acted or responded to potentially dramatic situations. I came up with some simple ways to do just that. I started asking myself if this issue was worth the headache, if the pros' outweighed the cons. Was I really going to RESPOND to stupidity, and if so; **HOW** was I going to respond? I learned to sum up a situation quickly, evaluate it, and then RE-EVALUATE it! If the "cons" outweighed the "pros'", well then; I would REVERSE! That means to put myself in the other person's position, to empathize. *"Is this going to happen and am I going to be responsible for it?"*

Look at it this way. Re-evaluate, Reverse, and Rejoice, or; React, Respond, and Regret! If you choose to do the first three, then you will find that you are behaving less like a savage and more like an adult. Now; I know that everybody cannot be held accountable for some of the situations that were thrust at them from "out of left field" as the saying goes; yet, **YOU** still have a choice on how the situation turns out for **YOU**! Try doing the first three R's and notice that you will not dwell on what could have been a stressful situation. Instead of being mad for two or three days about some drama that could have been avoided if you had just done the first three, you will be busy REJOICING because you were mature enough NOT to respond to SPDS (yours or the other person's).

So remember, RE-EVALUATE, REVERSE, AND REJOICE or REACT, RESPOND, AND REGRET! The choice is yours. Do you consider yourself to be "grown"? Think like it and then ***BEHAVE LIKE IT***!! Once again here are **some Do's** for you.

DO—Practice the first three R's.

DO—Learn to lower your voice! Here I go, stressing the importance of this thought a lot! I am originally from The Bronx, New York and was raised to cheer for the home team, so I am naturally a loud person (this comes from all those years cheering for The Yankees). People sometimes misunderstand me, because they think I am yelling at them. I really am not, but I didn't realize how loud my voice has become until last year.

Another instance of my SPDS rearing its ugly head: I am on a crowded train, and even though the young man that just took the seat that I was going to sit on didn't see my cane (I sometimes use a cane to walk now), I immediately made the comment *out loud* about the rudeness of today's youth. Well, needless to say; drama followed because the young man's mother; whom he was getting the seat for heard me and an argument ensued. All because I gave voice to my thoughts and they were heard by others.

Believe it or not, how loud you speak directly affects your mood. I had to practice speaking in a softer tone, and found that when you lower your voice, you feel better because being loud takes a lot of energy out of you. I'm serious. Not only do you sound better but, you feel good because no one can misunderstand you if you speak in a soft but clear tone of voice. Besides that, when you use your "inside voice" you'll find that people will listen more. No one wants to listen to a screeching alley cat!

Have you ever noticed that men tend to show more attention to the *"quiet"* one in your group, you know; the conservative one? Nine times out of ten, the man (or woman) you wind up in a relationship with is directly determined by the way you presented yourself when first speaking to them. Men; nor women "like" loud, rude "talkers". They tend to feel that you're always angry.

SPDS is the inappropriate behavior that affects you in so many different ways. Talking loudly is another symptom and represents your "ghetto" mentality. I am a firm believer in "ghetto is the state of your neighborhood, ***NOT*** your state of mind" Act like you have good sense, not like you keep up NONSENSE!! Better yet; act **AGE-APPROPRIATE**!!

YOU should never be seen out in public acting like someone's "CHICKEN HEAD BABY'S MAMA", at ANY AGE!!!! If you and the father of your kids are having a disagreement, only the two of you should know about it! Everyone on the bus, at the gas station, in the mall, in the grocery store, etc., does not need to know all your damn business! Also; **STOP** getting angry at passers-by, and asking what the hell are they looking at, because *you know **EXACTLY** why* they're staring! Lower your voice and in turn, lower others interest in what you are saying. You are in public after all.

If you are arguing with anyone on your cell phone, that person is not there for you to be yelling all your business anyway. Do this instead of arguing in public—tell the person you will call them back when you can talk privately, then hang up, turn your phone off or put it on vibrate, and handle the rest of your business.

NOW for some more Do's and Don'ts.

Don't—Forget any of the previous.

Don't—Forget to pray!

Don't—Forget that in order to improve yourself, you must first admit that you need to ADMIT that you need improvement!

Do—Remember to put GOD first and all things will be added unto you.

Do—Lower your voice in public!

Do—Make sure your behavior doesn't make you seem like less of an adult. GOD is watching! So is everybody else!

If you behave inappropriately; it is a direct negative reflection on your parents. You know your momma taught you better! Also; remember that once you turned 18, you were taught to be responsible for ALL of your actions, and anything you do will reflect your mindset. You say you're "grown", try to show it!!

Chapter 4: Whoah Momma!

Age-Appropriate behavior while out with your kids and at home!

I had my first child at sixteen years of age. By the time I was twenty-four, I had three more. Amazingly, I don't regret having any of my children. I do, however; regret not being able to wait until I was older to start raising a family. What does a sixteen year old know about life to teach to an infant? I had a lot of help from people, yet I didn't have the sense GOD gave a duck to raise myself; let alone my kids.

Now, when I was a fifteen year old; I behaved age-appropriately. I was in a good student in high school, had a little part time job, (another topic which will be discussed later in this and another chapter chapter), was on my school track, volley ball and debate teams, hung out with my "friends", and fought every day there was school in session! I was a teenager with **an attitude**! I was also confused, insecure, and had a Jerri-Curl! I was a "MEAN, LEAN Teenage Machine" and an ALIEN! I worried about teenage issues, behaved like a fifteen year old should. I didn't have a care in the world!

I also caught walking pneumonia! I had only had sex one time. You can imagine my surprise then; when 3 months later, my mom had to take me to the emergency room because I couldn't breathe and when the doctor came to give his diagnosis, he informed my alcoholic mother that she was to be a grandmother 6 months later! Oh and to get these prescriptions filled. The medicines were an anti-biotic to clear the infection from my lungs, and the other was for my pre-natal pills. I was so scared. How do you get pregnant, and not know it? I had some really tough choices to make.

I will never regret having my son. He grew up to be handsome, smart, and talented. I do regret NOT waiting until I was an adult to have a child. Well, technically; I had no choice. I was pregnant at fifteen and my biological mother was a devout Roman Catholic, (alcoholic, cigarette smoking, profane but still devout) and she made sure I couldn't get an abortion. She took my medical insurance card, my birth certificate, and my social security card and hid them, saying to me that we were not baby murderers and if I hadn't been so damned fast, I wouldn't need to think about killing a baby in the first damned place!

I admit, that I thought about abortion for about 10 seconds. Then, my teenage mind told me; "I can do this, I can raise a child on my own!" My mother had done it, so had my grandmother, and I felt assured that since they had been teenaged mothers, I could too. I "loved" his father, and I believed he loved me, too. He was the "bee's knees" to me. Eleven years older, fine as frog hair, and "hood rich". He was a drug dealer and I was his "littlest soldier". I would run away from time to time to help him do all his illegal business. (That part-time job I mentioned.) Needless to say, he was a real JERK! He was also married, had a few other kids with a few other young girls, and wound up in jail before my baby turned three months old.

I see first hand how a young girl can get so caught up in the "glamorous life". My son's father thought he was GOD's gift to any and EVERY vagina over the age of 13. He was sooo wrong!!! He caught me with the old "he's cute, he's paid, and he drives", you know; the old "23 skid-doo". My son and I couldn't depend on this jerk and our struggle was deep and hard. Very **_un-like_** the sex it took to create my precious gift. Even though his father was so much older than me, he was still a child mentally and emotionally. I didn't know what was in store for my baby and I, but even with limited knowledge; I was sure "the sperm donor" wouldn't be there in any regards.

I raised my baby boy on and off (because of my foster-care situation—I wrote another book discussing this in detail) for the first three years by myself. I received no help from anyone, not even my mom. I made plenty of "grown-up" decisions, and even more childish mistakes. I started smoking marijuana at the age of thirteen, and I only stopped during my pregnancies. (I have studied the topic of the medicinal properties of marijuana extensively. I started as a pot head, and grew into a "legalization of marijuana" advocate. Now I am strongly recommending NO KIND OF DRUG USE for anyone!) Mainly, I needed to tell you this because of the repercussions of more of my SPDS, this time while I was out with my children.

I strongly recommend NOT SMOKING WEED while you have to take your children out of the house! AT ANY AGE!! What you do when you're with the kids, the kids will do, even when they're NOT with you (especially, when they're not with you!) Do you remember the chapter on age-appropriate dressing? This is more important when you have kids. Well, I learned that lesson the hard way! Let's re-visit my 25th birthday.

I threw a party at one of Queens' biggest clubs in the 90's, The "Q" Club! I was a regular there and was friends with the resident party promoters. I also had the money to splurge on such an event. I also had four children under the age of 10. (* quick note: I sold a lot of personal property to get most of the money I used on that party, money that could have been spent on my children, but ; I was "GROWN" and NOT thinking about any kids). Now I can tell you that the party started at 10pm, lasted until 5; and was GREAT!!

The problem: I was wearing my party clothes when I had to drop my children off at the sitter. Using my twenty-five year old brain, I under-estimated the amount of time I needed to prepare on the day of the party. I was running three hours behind schedule and would have made my ride late to the party, so I decided to let the ride go ahead without me and I would take the bus. I also decided in my child's mentality to smoke a joint of some real strong weed, so I would already be woozy when I made my Grand Entrance! I was also high when I shopped for the "birthday" outfit earlier that day.

Do you remember the description of that outfit: The hot pink and black, leopard print bustier, over black booty shorts, and hot pink, patent leather, thigh-high stiletto boots? I even rocked hot pink stockings under black fishnets! I didn't understand that I wasn't sexy as much as I looked sluttish. I was 25, it was my birthday! I was "hot to trot, and fast in my ass" like my Grandma used to say!

Well ya'll, reality came quick that night! I put the kids in front of the T.V. so I could shower and dress. A cable station was showing a Julia Roberts marathon, and the kids were watching the opening scene in "Pretty Woman" when I was ready to leave the house. I walked four blocks to the bus stop, in high heels and booty shorts, with four kids at 10:30pm, on a Friday Night! My baby sitter lived up the street from the club, so I figured I wouldn't be to put out of my way!

My sitter was an elderly woman from Jamaica, West Indies. Her reaction to my attire told me everything I needed to know about how I REALLY looked! All she said was "Uum, nice boots", but the once over she gave me with her eyes said "now you're bugging!" My oldest daughter was only six years old at the time, and when she came to say goodnight, heard the boot comment and decided to "stick up" for me. "I think Mommy looks pretty", she said as she hugged me with those beautiful eyes that look like mine," just like the lady from the movie we was watching before we got here, Only PINK!"

Needless to say, I went to the party intent on being "GROWN", but in my high state of mind, I had forgotten to show my youngest son's father this very un-wise ensemble **BEFORE THE PARTY**! As soon as he saw me, all hell broke loose! "Tell me that the kids did NOT see you dressed like that", that's all he said and then took off his blazer and made me wear it all night! I think the security guards are the only people who saw that outfit. The next day, when I went to pick up my children, the sitter decided that I needed a "dressing down", a good talking too. She was very kind and gentle with me.

She offered me a cup of mint and orange tea (the recipe for that is in the back of this book) and told me to have a seat. She said in her most caring voice, "Munchie (my childhood nickname), you were just a little loud, a little too bold and a bit too YOUNG to be as undressed as you were last night. But it's your birthday and I understand you wanted to be sexy. I'm all for that, but did you really bring those children here, with you wearing that outfit? **YOU ARE A MOTHER FIRST**, so there is never a point in your life that it's okay for you to be OUTSIDE ANYWHERE AT ANY TIME DRESSED LIKE A HOOKER!! Don't you *CARE* what your kids will think?"

I was so caught off-guard by her comments that I really had to THINK like a G.A.W. My oldest son had been a little more than embarrassed to be seen with me the night before. I normally sit the children together, but my son sat two seats in front of me the whole 25 minutes we were on that bus, and then he walked ahead of me the rest of the way to the sitter's house with his head cast towards the ground, the whole way there. I was so high that I had not noticed how he was behaving, like he was ASHAMED of me!

That case of SPDS was only one of my many bouts with age-inappropriate dressing over the years, but it was by far the most awful and memorable. For my kids to view me as "pretty as the lady in the movie, only pink", put some things into perspective for me. The next time I went shopping for the "birthday outfit"; I took my son. I let him choose for me and I must say that his choice wasn't my preference; yet the outfit was nice. He was 14 then, and it was my 31st birthday. He chose cream colored pants and a matching knee length, sleeveless duster and a pretty chocolate and caramel shirt and flat heeled sandals to match. He even picked out my accessories. I looked like a thirty-one year old. When I asked him why so much material, he laughed a little and said "do I need to remind you of your 25th birthday outfit, PRETTY WOMAN?"

I laughed too, but inside I was HURT! 6 years had passed, but he would never forget that his MOTHER was dressed like a hooker for her birthday. Seeing me dressed like an extra from a Madonna video had traumatized my children and I wasn't aware of how much until that very moment. Since I was high on that birthday, I really couldn't see the long term effects my state of dress (or mind) would have on my children.

As I grew older, more of my SPDS would come back to bite me on the butt. My weed smoking in front of the children MORE than anything else! Every one of my four smokes weed now! This is something I tried to avoid over the years, using one of my mom's favorite sayings: DO AS I SAY, NOT WHAT I DO! Yet that proved to be futile, because how can you preach that to kids with a blunt in one hand, and booty shorts on? Reality sets in very quickly when your kids can give you lessons on morality.

When I was my children's ages, I felt betrayed by my mom's hypocritical sayings. I mean, how was I going to DO as she SAID any way? She was so drunk through the majority of my life that I barely understood what she was doing so great any way that I would **want** to do as she did. I grew up though and now I realize that she was a baby herself when she was barely raising me. My mom is 19 years older than me, and would have turned 60 this year if she had lived. I didn't realize that she wasn't really concerned with HOW she behaved in front of me when I was younger because SHE was still young herself. She was actually behaving *AGE-APPROPRIATE*. (I also secretly thank her for making me realize that NO ONE is UGLIER than: A LOUD, DRUNK WOMAN!) I miss her and I wish she could see that I wound up taking more of her advice than she prayed for.

When you have kids, AAB (age appropriate behavior) should be the first thing on your mind from the time you get your due-date from your doctor! You must remember that YOU are responsible for forming the life of the little person who shares more than your D.N.A. Children are a lot of things: curious, playful, fun and fantastic. They are also GREAT at perceiving everything you do as lessons to mimic. They are little sponges, ready to soak up information. Even as young as 4 or 5 months old, they are storing everything they see and hear for future reference to growing up.

Most adults think that children don't know anything about anything. How wrong you are if this is your philosophy! It's the other way around, YOU DON'T KNOW ANYTHING! If you are a mother of any age, you should definitely follow my advice. It will save you a lot of heartache in the long run. Now let's move on to the Do's and Don'ts.

DO: Think and re-think the choices you make BEFORE you carry out any action. Children learn from you first. What you do, they will do. Unless you have "super kids", baby geniuses that could TEACH you a thing or two about being a grown up!

Do: Talk honestly and openly (but remember you're speaking to children). They don't need to know ALL of your business! Adults need to exercise a bit more discretion when we discuss things with our kids. What exactly does a seven year old know about you going to the club last night and meeting the man that's in your bed at the moment? Choose carefully what you say to your kids. They may just repeat it at the most inopportune time. The kids weren't there when you were doing the dirt, so they don't need to be there AFTER the dirt has been done!

DO: LISTEN TO YOUR CHILDREN!! They can be brutally honest, so pay attention to what they say. They will let you know that they have been paying attention to your words and ACTIONS. Be prepared to answer some tough questions, and make sure that these answers are AGE-APPROPRIATE! Telling a five year old, "mommy has **NEEDS**" is NOT COOL OR APPROPRIATE!!

DO: Remember that for 18+ years, this child is using you as a role model. Are you looking forward to seeing your kid's name on a marquee, in lights? How about if it's over the entrance to the STRIP CLUB? Or hearing that your son is the star of a pornography film, (did you really raise "The NEW Long Dong Silver"?)

DO: Tell your partner (if you have one), about your exploits, so the kids DON'T beat you to it!

Example: your mate is out of town for the weekend, and you and your girls decide to have an "exhale" night. You all go to the male strip show, where you get drunk and tip the "fireman" $500. On Monday morning, the phone rings, while you're getting the kids ready for school. It's your best friend calling to discuss the weekend. **Do** call her back later or you risk missing the breakfast conversation between your kids and your mate. You get to the kitchen and the conversation goes from good morning to "hey honey, little Jr. just told me that you were pretty sloshed Friday night, and who is the fireman that put out your fire for $500?". Can you say "Uncomfortable situation"?

DO: Explain, without giving too much detail, that you had fun, just like the kids do, only you were doing fun things for "adults". You are a PARENT, ACT LIKE ONE!! Your kids ARE NOT YOUR AGE. Stop using them as therapists!

DON'T: tell your children you're going to "get your grove on". What does a minor know about "**GROOVE**"?

DON'T: LIE TO YOUR KIDS!! Santa Claus, The Easter Bunny, the Tooth Fairy, monsters under the bed that eat BAD children that don't eat their vegetables, etc., are for a child's imagination to grow, not for BRIBES! Don't tell your little ones "fancy stories" (lies), so they will go to bed early so you can "get your groove on"! First of all, kids aren't stupid. They figured out that Mommy doesn't know Santa personally, when they were 4. So YOU making empty threats, (Mommy is going to tell Santa to put coal in their stocking if they don't go bed right now); is totally MOOT!

DON'T : Chastise your children for telling THE TRUTH about your business! If it's YOUR business, it directly INVOLVES THEM BECAUSE THEY ARE YOURS!! Teach them how to MIND THEIR OWN DAMNED BUSINESS FROM THE START!! Then, you don't have to worry about Dad accidently finding out what you did while he was gone.

DON'T: Expect kids to understand that you have "needs". Just get a lock on your bedroom door, accompany it with a "Mommy only!" sign and teach them what that means, so they KNOW NOT TO KNOCK WHEN THEY SEE IT!

DON'T: Leave evidence of your "me and my mate's indiscretions" where the kids can find them! Your children will *not* understand why they should be watching the cartoon you bought for them for Christmas, but instead; Mommy is chasing Daddy around the room with a shredded, leather whip, or why Daddy has a ball in his mouth and is enjoying getting whipped! If you decide to tape you and your mate's encounters, label them clearly, then; LOCK THEM AWAY! It's *NOT* complicated at all, if you just take time to ACT LIKE YOU'RE "GROWN"!

DON'T: Act like you were never a child. At some point we were ALL kids. We all wanted to be like the "grown-ups" and do what the "big folks" did. When we became teens, we felt lied to by our parents. We all went through feeling that our parents lied to us at some point. We all had rebellious thoughts. Remember wishing that Mom got hit by a truck? Or trying to melt into a puddle or become invisible when Dad tried to kiss you good-bye when he dropped you off at school? News flash: so did your parents and so will your kids. So grow the ___up, and remember that you WERE A CHILD ONCE!

Here's a "good" DO for you. DO: Invest in a couple of bath robes. I don't mean the pretty peignoir that came with the camisole you bought one Valentine's Day a few years ago. I mean a sturdy, terry cloth number, the one you'd put on to answer the door if you're not dressed and the doorbell rings or grab to throw on if the kids knock while you are "busy". As a matter of fact, buy two, one for after your shower or bath and one just for covering purposes. Just remember that if your kids are home, they will more than not use whatever bathroom is available. It can traumatize a kid to see Mom running from the bathroom to her bedroom butt-naked, at 3am in the morning! Buy matching slippers too. That way, you're covered and a benefit of wearing a robe is that you will eventually have to get dressed. (You can also hide that "little pretty pink thing" you picked up at VS).

Now one last DON'T. DON'T: Under any circumstances, forget that your "inner freak" should only be displayed for your mate! Only at an APPROPRIATE time, like when the kids are out of the house for at least 3 or 4 hours, or away at Grandma's for the weekend or at camp, etc . . . ! You get the idea. I am not saying **to not** have relations with the kids at home, I am however; diligently reminding you of the old saying "every closed eye ain't sleep and every good-bye ain't gone"!

Unless you want your 3 year old mimicking your sounds of pleasure, try to keep your voice down when you and your partner are "doing the do" as my mom used to say. Remember, Age-Appropriate behavior starts with you teaching your kids how to ACT their age. I understand that it's your house, but; remember the kids live there too. This leads us directly to the next chapter entitled "You're Grown, So Buy Your Own!"

*(By the way, if you are a single mom; **_please stop_** letting these kids refer to your boyfriends as "Uncle" and "Daddy". If you're a homosexual female, **NEVER should a child be heard** CALLING YOU DADDY!! If you are **_truly a lesbian_**, then **you KNOW** you are a female and don't want any one calling you "DADDY" anyway, because you are **NOT A MAN**!!! Just be yourself, and read chapter 8. I wrote that chapter just for my lesbian sisters!)

CHAPTER 5: YOU'RE GROWN SO BUY YOUR OWN!!!

Scenario: You turned 18 and you and your parents don't see eye to eye on anything. Every 30 seconds, MOM is yelling and telling you 'Don't' about something. Don't drink all the milk, don't leave dirty dishes in HER sink, don't leave towels on HER floor, DON'T, DON'T, DON'T, do anything she doesn't approve of in HER HOUSE!

You get so fed-up that you scramble up some money and move out. I mean, after all; *YOU* are *"GROWN"*, right? WRONG! In this day and age, more adults are living with their parents. Because of the inflation and recession, financial burdens can be shared between the adult members of a household to lighten every one's load. You're moving back in with your parents is supposed to ease burdens, NOT to cause more stress.

I moved back in with my mother when I was thirty-one. I really needed my mom's emotional support. What I **didn't** need was the "MOTHER-MOUTH", or the yakking all day about how she "HAD TOLD ME SO". I was just getting out of an abusive relationship, my kids were turning into aliens, (they were in age order 15, 12, 11, and 9), and I was really going through some rough patches. I was yelling at everybody, and very angry at myself for putting my kids through one of the worst cases of SPDS I ever suffered.

What I also *DIDN'T need* was to be: yelling how "GROWN" I was, or throwing up in my MOTHER'S face how I was contributing to her household financially, and not listening to a GROWNER-THAN-ME-ASSED-WOMAN teaching me that I wasn't Behaving Appropriately! Honey, I was too grown and so wrong! In my mother's house, you made breakfast, lunch and dinner for the whole household at least three nights a week, but for your kids, EVERY DAMNED DAY!! She was the

Grandma, but **YOU ARE THOSE KIDS MOTHER**!! Mom didn't lie down and make those babies.

My mother had an opinion on everything. "You better catch that little fast tail gal, before you become a grandmother before you turn 40, and tell that damn boy to pull up his pants, don't nobody want to see his narrow ass!" My all-time favorite: "When are you moving into your own place again? I mean I love you, but you're supposed to be "grown"? I couldn't even borrow $20 from her and I was paying half the bills! If she did lend it to me, I had to pay it back the same day. If I was three minutes late in paying her back, I heard about it for weeks after, which would piss me off, of course!

What could I say about it though? She was right, like years of life experience tends to be. If I was remotely comfortable in my previous circumstance, I wouldn't be back in HER house. That's the whole point. Once you pay for your own stuff, you begin to understand why mothers seem like they have so many "MOMMY RULES". My mom taught me how to curse creatively and discipline my kids without scarring them by putting "grown-up" situations into their lives. When I was misbehaving as a child, I got my ass whipped! Nothing changed because I turned 31. One of her favorite sayings was specifically for me. "GIRL, shut the __UP, and feed them babies!"

She drove me crazy! Then I lost her, and gained some personal wisdom which helped with my personal growth. Before she died, I promised my mother that I would try to better myself and become the woman she envisioned when I was born. I started having conversations with GOD and myself. I had to breakthrough so I could begin healing and growing up. I did a lot of self-evaluation, and began slowly changing into a mature young lady.

I began acting age-appropriate. I started to see the inner strength my mom told me we all have as humans. I started praying in earnest, I stopped playing "the girl with the lukewarm faith". I try to behave appropriately at all times. *I fail* more than I care to admit, but that just makes my little successes all the more sweet!

I fail, but I am learning to continue to move forward instead of reverting to my old way of thinking more often now. I started with baby steps and every step counts!

I began looking at "the man in the mirror" (miss you much, Michael). I learned to be appreciative of "my own stuff". "Pay for your own shit" probably comes out of my mouth more now that my kids are mostly legal aged. I know it stayed coming out of every body's mother's mouth that I knew, especially my own!

If you want to know if you are age-appropriately behaved, ask your mom (or any one's mom) and she'll definitely tell you. If you have one question, Mom has **_all_** the answers! Whether it's the solutions to global warming, ending wars, famine and disease or how to make Grandma's baked macaroni and cheese, and why that big head, motorcycle riding, cigarette-smoking bad boy wasn't good enough for her baby, you name it and she has the answer! Mom knows EVERYTHING!

Paying for your own means a lot more than you may think. You first need to understand that if your things mean something to you, you will definitely appreciate them more if something happens to them. You gain a better understanding of WHY you could never "DO" anything in your parents' house. Do you let people just run all over your home, or let other people's children tear up your kids' toys? We all know the answer to that. Hell NO! If you have your own, people have to respect your rules.

Move out on your own again and I promise you, the lesson intended will be learned quickly. If you still can't afford to move; try learning to RESPECT other people's rules like you would want yours respected! Also, **_please STOP COMPLAINING_** about what other people won't do for you! Do it yourself, and you won't have to be angry because "they" won't do for you what your "grown" behind should have already done. Following someone else's rules teaches us to make up our own rules, and set our own boundaries in our OWN lives. Maturity is learning to value what little bit you may have and treating it like it's the CROWN JEWELS, because that's how you want others to treat it.

So, have some empathy for Mom. This living arrangement is supposed to be beneficial for everyone involved, and try to remember that your parents have already raised you. Their job was done the minute you tried to run off with that "bad boy" your mom tried to warn you about and you yelled "I'm GROWN, I can make MY OWN DECISIONS"! Now here you are, 35 years old; still yelling about how GROWN you are, yet you're living under your parent's roof, still mooching off of them. Stop talking about being "grown" and act like it!

You have loudly told anyone that will listen that you're an adult, that you can do what you want. Well, if you're so GROWN, BUY YOUR OWN!! If you had done your job in the first place, you wouldn't have had to move back in with your folks. So, show some respect to others and they will show you some in kind.

*(A personal thought: try to make the best of the situation by working WITH your folks instead of against their rules. Have a talk with them, not an argument; and explain that you need them to respect your boundaries, too. If you moved back in to take care of your aging parents, be GRATEFUL that you still have them to take care of. My mom used to tell me that you're once an adult, but twice a child. That means once you've grown up, you are no-one's responsibility, but once you grow "OLD", you are someone's responsibility again. Now your parents are your charges. Take good care of them, because they took good care of YOU!)

CHAPTER 6: HANDLE YOUR OWN BIZ, MIZZ!

Now ladies and gents, (mostly Ladies); I'd like to switch up the topics for a moment. I'd like for you to reflect on your personal relationships, specifically your romantic relationships. If you are over thirty and you are still referring to your significant other as "my boyfriend" or, "my old man", then you really need to rethink the definitions of these titles you give your mate. With more than 60% of today's marriages ending in divorce in the first 3-5 years, longer engagements are definitely recommended. Yet; at the same time, if you've been in a romantic relationship with the same person since the 10th grade, and twenty years have gone by and you have children with this person and you live together; introducing this person as "my man", or "my boo" or my all-time favorite: "my special friend" is not beneficial to either of you!

If anything, it shows that you have commitment issues. A 20-year relationship is a blessing. Some people shouldn't be married and will stay for "the kids" or "he's the one that pays the bills" or again, another favorite: the house is in BOTH of our names! Now, I have been married twice (legally), and have been engaged to the same man for almost ten years. We are in no rush to get legally wed, why should we be; to make other people happy?

That's not going happen, because we are sticking to our 10-year rule. If we can live, laugh, and LOVE together for ten years, then we can get married and stay together for twenty more! We have been acting married for the last 8 and a half years anyway, and when we introduce each other to others, we say "this is my husband/wife to be" or just my husband/wife. We are very happy to do this because we truly have something special and very rare: We LOVE each other!

We do have a problem though. Our mutual friends and family members want us to get legally married, and are constantly badgering us to make it "legal" or as one of my cousins always says; "make it right in GOD's eyes so HE can continue to bless you". That translates to: get married so we can be a part of your B.I.Z!! Now my mate and I are still trying to work out the "kinks" in our relationship, making sure to examine our compatibility so we don't make mistakes in the future that can embitter us towards each other. We have our "ups and downs and in-betweens" just like every other couple we know. We also don't care what other people think about our relationship status.

We don't pay any of the so-called "good advice" any mind at all. What the problem that we both have is other people trying to "Handle Our BIZ"! When I started this book, I decided to ask one of my "friends" why it was so important to other people what was going on in my personal life, why my marital status was so essential to them. Before I give her response, let me tell you a little bit of HER personal business. She is an attractive, intelligent, college educated, morally up-right, over-40-year old, who has two adult children and has never had her own home.

When we were younger, she was just as bad at behaving age-appropriate as I was. Speed up twenty years. I've progressed and matured, found real love (finally) and at the start of my relationship with him, she was so "happy" for me. So it shocked me when I told her we had set a date and all of a sudden, she didn't want us to get married. When I posed the "why is my marital status" question, she said that I had made wrong choices in the past and she didn't want to see me hurt again. Now please understand that I love her for that, but; how do you take marital advice from someone who has never been married, ever? As far as I know, she's never had a meaningful relationship that lasted more than a year before she found out that it wasn't going to be like the movies and books said it was. But advise me; she did. My husband-to-be doesn't care about her "advice" though. He thinks she's perpetuating drama because she's jealous. After the 30 minute argument she and I had about her feelings on our relationship, I tend to agree with him.

This is where the problem of other people's opinions comes into play. We are totally in love with each other and nobody but us will be getting married. The only thing is, that when we marry each other; we will also be "marrying" one another's family and friends. Now all of my folks adore him, they say he is the best thing that has ever happened to me. I agree. She did too, until we set a date.

Now every conversation she and I have turns into an argument, complete with yelling and cursing. We argue about all of my relationships, past and present.

Now, "Sistah" I love you, but after 25 years of failed relationships, I think I've learned a few valuable lessons so that I can keep this husband. I was given ample opportunity to "get me right" for the man that GOD sent to love and honor me. I have learned, matured and behave in a manner that is much more adult since my first marriage when I was 19, and my second marriage when I was 30. It's not like she has slept with him, to know anything about our business anyway.

See you all, I am NOT a "sharer". When I was younger, **all** of my business was **all** of my people's business. I stopped divulging relationship stories after a few in-appropriate situations happened concerning my so-called mates, and my so-called friends.

I stopped talking about my business, and involving other people into it as well. Now most of you ladies are saying "I don't tell people my business" and you might not. Most women (notice I said WOMEN) don't anymore. Admit though, that at one time or another; you would call your girls if your mate was bugging out, wilding out, or sometimes just going out!

In chapter 1, we discussed identifying Self-Perpetuated Drama Syndrome (or SPDS), and some of the symptoms. One was age-inappropriate behavior. Another is what I like to call "Not handling your **business-itis**". You can tell if you have SPDS if you suffer with this, too. Here are a few questions to ask yourself so that you can battle this particular "**ITIS**".

1. Do you discuss your personal relationship with your friends?
2. Do any of your friends offer advice on that relationship, without being asked for it?
3. Does the advice come from a friend in a successful relationship?
4. Does the advice given cause arguments between you and your friends?
5. Does this advice cause arguments between you and your mate?
6. Is any of this un-solicited advice beneficial to your relationship?
7. Is this advice being given by a single friend?
8. When was the last time that this friend was in a successful relationship?

9. Why aren't they in one now?
10. Do you always seek advice from others? And if so; when are YOU GOING TO LEARN TO ACT AGE-APPROPRIATE AND DEAL WITH YOUR OWN DAMNED ISSUES??!!??

If you answered yes to any of the "yes or no" questions, then that last question is JUST FOR YOU! Why would you tell any of your business to your friends? Don't you have a mind of your own? Why would you take relationship advice from single people, or people who can't maintain a good relationship? If they **KNEW** how to "help" you, why couldn't they help themselves?

I am not saying that **ALL of your friends** mean you harm. I'm just trying to get across to you that although some might have your benefit at heart, others aren't trying to help you. These are the ones with the issues in their own lives that they can't resolve and **your business** is a distraction for them. It gives them a sense of **power** to try to "help" you with your business, because they have no CONTROL over their own.

Example: You and your single friends used to do EVERYTHING together, going out to dinner, to the movies, to the club, etc. Then you found a mate and so do they. Now everything is done in pairs. That is until her mate and she find out they aren't compatible after all. Your relationship is going strong, and your love life is spectacular.

Now you're still in "wife" mode, but she's single AGAIN, so she becomes angry with you that you are not LONELY. She makes little "hater" comments, and tries to "guilt" you into forgetting that you are in a committed relationship. You are supposed to forget your mate and go back to being "single" minded. Where does that leave the state of the relationship you're in? She is miserable and because you're not miserable, she starts pointing out ALL of your mate's "faults".

She claims to have "noticed" all these things wrong with him "before"; but you were just so happy, that she didn't want to upset you because she's your "friend". SURE! RIGHT! Okay, so what do you do now? Do you leave your working relationship based on HER advice? Or do you realize it's a jealousy thing on her behalf and STOP messing with her? AND; if you keep both relationships, how do you keep your mate and your friend separate? Believe me when I say that the problem, although it seems like a difficult one; is actually very simple. How long you've been friends with this 'PARAGON' of sisterhood shouldn't even cross your mind.

As a matter of fact, neither should your relationship with your mate. The problem is handling your friend's SPDS with adequate action without causing any for yourself. If this is not your problem or you are still behaving like a child by refusing to take advice on how to cure your SPDS then; by all means PLEASE put this book down,(or turn to what applies to you) and get ready to make a TOUGH LOVE CHOICE! If you truly want to end this very unnecessary problem, then keep reading.

In my own life, I have utilized 2 simple steps to stop the nonsense. These two steps will put a new perspective on your friendship and your relationship. Step one: REMOVE THIS SO-CALLED FRIEND FROM YOUR CIRCLE. Step two: DON'T INVITE HER BACK IN! MEANING: NONE OF YOUR BUSINESS IS HER'S, SO DON'T DISCUSS IT WITH HER EVER AGAIN!! See how simple this is. Don't make up with her. Her opinion is what caused your rift to begin with. Show her that it really doesn't do either of you good to argue about what you do.

Now there is a third step, but this is only for those of you whose "friends" will want to fight ending the friendship. Just keep her and your mate completely separated. Don't invite them to the same functions, don't set up "mediations", and don't treat her like her feelings are more important than yours. If you are related by blood, blood is thicker than water, but water is better for you; if you can understand that.

Also; NOT playing the "what do you think I should do about . . . ." Game is definitely an option. I mean, you wouldn't have to get rid of either your mate or her if you just don't share your business in the first place. I know this sounds difficult, but really ladies, it's only as hard to accomplish as YOU allow it to be. If you are following the Do's and Don'ts of age-appropriate behavior that I have been giving, you'll find that you don't even have time to dwell on such trivial matters or THE DRAMA!

Little ant hills or big mountains, the choice is yours. If you opt to stop being her friend, it may sting a little for a while. If you choose to break up with your mate, you just gave someone else power over you. She will become your enemy because you will resent her interference. In the long run, you will have caused undo heartache, (to the mate and yourself); while she is happy to be miserable with your company.

Keeping your business to yourself takes practice. The BIBLE says; "Whoso keepeth his mouth and his tongue keepeth his soul from troubles" and that a "fool uttereth his mind: but a wise man keepeth it in till afterwards" (Proverbs 21:23, Proverbs29:11). So unless you NEED to tell someone your business, (if you're being beaten by your mate for example, then RUN, don't walk and tell on that coward—male OR female!) keep your personal relationship private.

Don't give someone the ammunition to shoot you in the back. Stop telling your folks all about you and yours! HANDLE YOUR OWN BIZ, MISS! If you follow my advice, but still need to talk to someone about your issues, call a professional and make an appointment to go to therapy. A mental health counselor is trained to listen, not judge and will help you to find the best solutions that YOU will come up with for your own problems.

I have been in counseling for a few years, on and off; and I find that I am more stressed when I am not seeing my therapist. If you think that only "crazy people" seek a mental health professional when they need to talk and can't do it with their "friends", well sweetie; YOU are the CRAZY one and definitely need to seek help! If you just can't seem to wrap your mind around telling a total stranger your business, there is ALWAYS GOD!! HE will NEVER FAIL YOU!!!

CHAPTER 7: THE JEALOUSY MUST END!!

We have covered a couple of really good topics on our road to self-enlightenment. Let's touch on one that might cause a few uncomfortable emotions. Jealousy or what I call "the poor man's snobbery" seems to be running rampant, especially amongst women of my generation (if you were born between 1965-1975).

In chapter 2, we discussed "She". It is apparent that "she" has low self-esteem. That's because, in her heart; she views herself as so invisible that she has to 'stand out'. The fact that you noticed her and have any emotion besides "none of my business" shows that you judged her. This is considered to be wrong. Now if you noticed her, and felt a little jealous, then your unwarranted anger is explainable. You suffer with low self-esteem as well and you felt a kindred spirit within her.

Why would you be jealous of her, right? I mean, look how she's dressed after all. To you, her appearance is jacked up. Even if you're wearing the same outfit, you still feel like she doesn't look good. I have a few signs to give you to look for if you think you may be envious of someone else. I also need to tell you the definition of "jealous". The word jealous means: "feeling envy at another person's situation or possessions." Example: "I am jealous of your beautiful home", or "you're jealous of the fact that we both know I look better than you in this outfit!"

Here are the signs you should look for (in yourself), to know if your jealous.
1) When you saw "her" and thought anything about her appearance that wasn't empathy.
2) If your confidence level is low, and you secretly wish you had that much confidence.

3) When your outfit matches hers, and you KNOW she looks better in it than you!

You see; a lot of people suffer with low self-esteem. Not just women, either. We are focusing on women now. Low self-esteem is "the feeling that you are not worthy to benefit from your own self-worth" or in simpler terms, YOU don't LIKE YOURSELF. If you have low self-esteem, "She" should not have affected you at all. SPDS due to low self-esteem is caused by a lot of different factors. A few are: suffering abuse of any form, rejection by an "attractive" individual, being told constantly you can't do any better, etc.

Some of us were taught to have a low self-view at our parent's homes, with our parents trying to teach us humbleness and going to far. It doesn't matter where you picked this up, so long as you PUT IT BACK DOWN again. SO; you don't think you're worth much, hunh? What do you intend to do about it? You know I have an opinion on this, too. Here are a few tips that may help you raise your level of self-esteem, allow you to stop being jealous of others, and teach you some techniques to avoid future drama because of your own self-view.

First, take a deep breath, and clear your mind. This will calm your nerves. Next, pray that GOD gives you a clear inner-sight, removing the ability to judge yourself. After that, take off all of your clothes, stand in front of a full length mirror and really look at yourself. Write down everything you see that you don't like about your physical appearance; "my butt is too flat, my eyes are crossed, my lips are too thin", etcetera. Now get dressed. Then look at your list and hit your knees and pray for a content and peaceful view of yourself.

Ask GOD to forgive you for being so critical of what HE created and for a removal of non-essential obstacles that were placed in front of you either by you or another person. Ask to be given the wisdom to know when you're going to make self-critical statement about yourself. (I don't like this or that about myself). Ask for the strength to stop yourself from making that statement. Now thank HIM for creating you, and get up from the floor, and KNOW that even if you don't feel you're worth it, that HE knows you are!

GOD, in HIS infinite wisdom; gave you the power to become "that which is good in HIS sight". He designed you with a purpose in mind for you. Like the old saying goes;" GOD DON'T MAKE NO JUNK"! Now sit down with your list and for every one thing you see wrong, try to put two things that you like about yourself down next to them. Lastly, focus on and enjoy the GOOD THINGS about you! Be honest about it, too. Since you are your biggest critic, you will be doing these simple exercises a few times a week to get the full benefits.

If you are the only basis for your own self-view, remember that you're going to be harder on your views of you than anyone else. Give yourself a chance to approve of something about you. Ask for guidance in navigating the low self-worth a little further up-stream, towards the positive aspects of yourself. In the great scheme of life, we were all given gifts that make us individuals. "A view from above" is what is needed to raise your self-esteem. When you learn to accept who you are and what is right with you, you will notice that the things you don't like on that list are going to become unimportant over time, and that the things you like will increase three-fold.

When you learn to view yourself from the "inside", you'll find that you'll become less critical of yourself and other people as well. If you only "see" your faults, you will only get faulty results. Learn to focus on the positive, and not the "fuckery"! Get it together, girl! View your strengths as weaknesses that got stronger, because that's exactly what they are! Realize that you were created for a purpose that was GOD given, and that is a good thing.

You have fortitude, so use it to make your fortune. You read your horoscope every day. Instead of listening to what the stars have to say about you, you should bear witness to what YOU want to happen in your future! Stop worrying about "her" and "she". Stop worrying about everything, period! If you worry, you get wrinkles and if you feel you look older than what you are because you have wrinkles, know that YOU have the power to change your appearance. Buy some anti-aging wrinkle removal cream and keep a happy view of yourself.

See yourself in a more positive light. See your character's GOOD SIDE as a good thing. STOP Down TALKING YOURSELF, PLEASE! No need to be jealous of "her". She has enough self-esteem to be seen in public "dressed like that". Instead of jealousy judging her, smile a genuine smile at her creativity and keep going about your business. You will know when you are no longer jealous when you can do this and come away from "her" knowing that you are confident in your age-appropriate attire, attitude and behavior!

Maybe "she" will look at you and think, "I know I look better than HER in this outfit"; maybe not. One thing is for certain though. You won't be affected by "her" once all you can see is the POSITIVE changes in *you*. You will be more than willing to teach her a thing or two about having HIGH SELF-ESTEEM. Then, she will get a glimmer of hope where she is concerned, because she'll see your inner peace, and wonder why you seem so happy.

If she asks you where you got those shoes, for instance; by all means tell her! Then recommend this book, tell her GOD bless her and finish your day knowing you may have helped someone else's self-view. By the way, if you help someone else with an issue that you used to have, that's YOU being a GOOD PERSON, so make sure to ADD THAT TO YOUR LIST!

*Now we are getting ready to move on to the next few chapters, but first I would like for you to answer a few questions for yourself.

1) Do you listen to what other people say about you?
2) Do you take their comments and internalize them?
3) If the answer to that is yes, WHY?
4) Do you love yourself, with all the good and bad traits?
5) Do you know that no-one can love you if you don't love yourself and accept who you are personally?

Remember: GOD DON'T MAKE NO JUNK!!!

Chapter 8: Am I Sexy Enough To Keep HIM?

You have a BIG Date tonight. You have been single a long time, and now you've met a person you'd like to be social with. You're standing in front of the closet, most of whose contents are on the bed because you can't make up your mind on what to wear. You just took a shower ten minutes ago, yet; you're sweating because you're nervous. Insert deep breath here, and stand still for a minute. Think about where your head is at. Then calm down and make wise, age-appropriate choices in your outfit.

Many of us have been in this situation. Am I sexy enough? Will he/she like my physical appearance or is this color ok on me, or why didn't I buy the other dress? I have a quick question for you. What were you wearing when you met this person and where are you going on the date? Using my advice as a guideline can ensure that not only will you be "sexy" enough to go out with this person, but; you will also learn how to keep them if this date works out.

I have not been single more than a year since I started dating. I have been married twice and am engaged now. I explained a couple of chapters ago why I am engaged now, and why both of my former marriages failed. A part of my initial problem was discussed last chapter. I suffered with low self-esteem. I have been in my current relationship for almost 9 years, and my future husband and I have a thing we do every day. (Besides pray together). Every day since the start of our relationship, my husband-to-be says "good morning, Beautiful" and my response is always "good morning, Handsome".

We started this by accident. It became "our thing" after doing it every morning for a few weeks. We do it after the bad arguments the night before, if we went to bed at all, winter, spring, summer, and fall for 8 years straight. It helps that we're still in love. I have been in a few relationships over the last twenty-five years that had me standing in front of my closet, sweating. One day I decided that instead of wondering if I was sexy enough for the potential mate, I was just going to be myself and put on a clean pair of jeans, a pretty top, and dress these up with some cute shoes and accessories.

I didn't even wear make-up. Just threw some eye-liner on and my ever present lip-gloss, sprayed a little of my favorite fragrance on my pulse points, grabbed my pocketbook and was out the door. I had one of the best dates ever! The point is I wasn't worrying about what he thought of me, if I was sexy enough for him, because I was too busy being ***comfortable in and with myself*** to worry about anything except having an enjoyable time. It turned out that he was nervous about the same thing I was originally and we have been in the same relationship for almost ten years!

I love the fact that men can wear whatever they want, where and whenever they want. If they wear suits to work, they have suits for that specific purpose. If they only wear jeans and tee shirts, they have specific places they wear them. They use the weather to determine what to wear. That's why most first dates are something casual, so they don't have to wear a tie. Most men are comfortable with themselves and I promise you, if he wants to take you out, he'll tell you what to wear by his choice of location. If he chooses dinner and a movie, you know to wear dinner and movie clothes. If you're going to the opera or ballet, you know to wear this type of clothes. Going dancing? Put on your dancing shoes. See the pattern? If we spent more time knowing for ourselves that we're sexy, we wouldn't be nervous about what he thinks. See ladies, sexy is internal first, meaning you have to feel like you're sexy enough for you in order to be viewed as such by others.

My favorite thing to do for myself is play a game I call—"how sexy am I today?" I play this game every morning, while I brush my teeth. I make sure that I ask myself this question before I get dressed, because the answer helps me to choose my clothes for the day. It also gives me a self-esteem boost, because I have to really think about what I am going to do to **NOT** have a day riddled with SPDS. Depending on what I have planned for the day, that one question can have many answers.

The one answer that always remains constant is "I am at my sexiest point in my life, because I love me". Then I follow that up with "what outfit matches my sexiness and my business today?" This is so I don't over-do it, or under-do-it, and run the risk of having a bad day. I then, pick out my outfit and get dressed. I go about my daily business and tend to have a great day!

The reason I play this game with myself is so that I remember that if I don't think I am sexy enough for myself, then I risk not being sexy enough for anyone else. How can I expect for another person to think anything about me that is positive, if I can't view myself with the same positive thought? I have to love me enough so that other people can treat me like I am loved by them. If I gave myself the attention I choose to get from "him", I wouldn't have to wonder if I am "enough of . . ." anything for anyone else.

This is the shortest chapter in this book, because it doesn't take long to summarize the previous chapters. I have learned that "self-love" is the only love that really matters. All my life I have heard people say; "it doesn't matter what other people think of you, it's what you think of yourself that matters". I always thought: easier said than done. I found out that while on the road to self-improvement, other people's opinions are just that—OTHER PEOPLE'S OPINIONS! I can't allow what other's think to guide my journey to betterment.

If I had a penny for every time someone else's opinion factored into to my SPDS, I would be a billionaire! I was so in-appropriately behaved at one point in my life, that I even sold my body for money and was PROUD of it. My low self-view then told me that I was "GROWN", that even though my "customers" were all ex-mates, I could do what I wanted with no retribution because "THEY" thought I was sexy. I remember telling a friend of mine not too long ago that I couldn't care less what they thought about how I was supporting myself. What I was really saying was that I didn't think I was SEXY to others and that all that mattered to me was that these former lovers still did think so.

Now I am not saying that the solution to prostitution is to read this or any other book. In fact, I learned a lot from being paid to do something I am so experienced in. I enjoyed the fantasy of being a paid whore. I built myself up to believe that prostitution was a game, and I was a winner because these men still wanted me sexually, and that even though our relationship used to be personal, now it was just business. Secretly, I cried each time because; I felt like all they ever wanted was sex from me. I was correct in my feeling this way since that *IS* all they wanted from me. I gave in to the pressures of my own low self-view because I wanted to be viewed as still attractive to these men. (I only had three customers, but I was convinced that I could put a price on my most precious gift and get revenge for the failed relationships at the same time). I was very wrong!

Now, believe me when I say I know that I am worth every dime I charged for my cookie, yet; the pay never was worth the pain I suffered by not having enough of a positive self-view. If my self-esteem was higher at that time, I would have charged more! I am just joking about that "charging more" bit. I was trying to make the point that when you believe you are worthless, you can't accept that "priceless" and "worthless" are NOT the SAME.

I have learned to view myself as PRICELESS. This means I have come to the understanding that my love is so special to ME, that THERE IS NO PRICE that anyone can afford to PAY for this! I am no longer selling my cookie. I found a permanent buyer who holds the exclusive bill of sale for the product I was offering: ME! I treat myself so well that I would marry myself if I could; because after GOD, I am the only one who loves me to the limit! There is not much I wouldn't do for MYSELF. I thank GOD every day for sending me "THE ONE", and he's thankful for me as well. I am MORE than appreciative that GOD DIDN'T MAKE NO JUNK WHEN HE MADE ME!

SO, do I think I am sexy enough for him? DAMN RIGHT I AM! Do other people think I am sexy enough for them? Who cares? I am sexy because I think I am and nobody can take that from me. If my soon-to-be husband were to leave me today, I would be hurt of course; but as long as I have GOD as my inner-mirror, I will never have to revert to in-appropriate behavior to see myself as a "good catch" again. I am SEXY, and I know this because I told me so.

So ladies, the moral of this story is to explain that ONLY YOUR thoughts of you matter. Think Positive things about you and see if others don't eventually see the "Sexy" you as well. If they don't see it, that's their problem!

*(Now, here's the "am I sexy enough" game. Please feel free to edit this to suit your own needs. After you wake up and Thank GOD for your life, go look in the bathroom mirror. As you stand there brushing your teeth, ask yourself any question you can come up with pertaining to your self-esteem. Now give yourself until the count of five before you answer the question: am I sexy enough or am I smart enough, etc. After the count of five, answer the question honestly. If your G.P.A. is 4.5, then your answer should always be "yes, and today I show how smart I am by my choices". If you look like a super model, you're going to focus on your INNER-BEAUTY, so your answer should reflect this. If you look nice in your clothes, your answer should be fashion related. Get the idea? Good. Let's move on.)

Chapter 9: You Are A Woman, So You Can't Be The Daddy!!

Now this chapter is dedicated strictly to my sisters that are living an "alternative lifestyle". By the time I am through with this chapter, I am probably going to have to defend my thoughts to every aggressive, homosexual female out there, but I am never scared to voice my thoughts, because I am correct and my thoughts are just that: MINE. If I didn't speak on this new phenomenon of "everybody is gay", I'd be a hypocrite of the worst sort, because I have been in a few same-sex relationships over the 25 years I have been dating.

These relationships never lasted longer than a "freak episode" for me because in my heart I know I AM NOT GAY! I can say however; that I appreciate a butt as big as mine and since I come from a long line of women with big breasts, I like breasts. This is not a problem for me, because I have come to realize that I enjoy sex with men more, so I may glance at a female I think is attractive, but I won't make any advances. I might even flirt a little, but it won't go any further than that. I am engaged to a great guy, and I take that very seriously. I also have four children, and two grandchildren, hence the need to explore this new "trend" of women calling other women "DADDY", and allowing the children to do so as well.

I explained my bi-sexuality because I need to get a message across to a few of the aggressive females that I have been speaking with concerning the children in their lives. After having interviewed a few of these ladies, I also came up with a solution to keeping SPDS from affecting the kids in their lives. First let's talk about what it really means to be a "lesbian". The dictionary says that a lesbian "is a woman who enjoys and engages in sexual behaviors strictly with other women"

The dictionary also lists the word "father" as the "male head of household". Now, please forgive me if I am wrong, but if the word "father" states that the person who is also called "Dad, Daddy, Pop, etc." is a MALE, and males are identified by their penis, then a lesbian cannot physically be a "father". Why is this so important to me, you may be asking. In the past couple of months, I have spoken to a few lesbians concerning why they are allowing their children to call their mates "Daddy". The answers astounded me and also started a couple of really bad arguments.

I don't believe that if you are in a same-sex relationship that this alone should justify the titles assigned to the partners in that relationship. If there are two homosexual men in a relationship, and there are children in the picture, do the partners allow the children to call one of them "Mother"? No, because even the partner who is considered the feminine one knows he is not a FEMALE! So after questioning ten lesbians, both Aggressive and Femme, ranging in age from 18-50, I came to the conclusion that the children involved in this kind of household where masculine titles are enforced, are being needlessly confused.

I decided to speak about it. I asked 5 questions to my group of homosexual women. Since they are so diverse in age, race and economic status, I figured that their answers would be just as diverse. I was wrong. I will list the questions below and hope that if you are a female in a same-sex relationship and reading this, that you will come to understand that the examples you set for the kids is helping to mold them into adults.

The questions are: Do you identify with feminine tendencies more than your masculine tendencies? 2) Do you approve of AG's "posing" as men? If so, do you consider this to be normal behavior for an aggressive female or just "penis envy"? 3) Do you now, or have you ever allowed your mate to call you "Daddy"? 4) Do you have children, and if so what do they refer to your mate as and why? 5) Do you approve of lesbians that allow their kids to call another woman by a male title and if not, why?

For the answers I was given, I chose 3 of my subjects because their answers were the most insightful. Their answers were also so different from each other's, and from the other ladies that I had to expound on them further. For this topic I will call my girls "Lucy, Gwen, and Sonia". I still am not using real names so as not to upset anyone any more than necessary to state my points.

Let's start with Lucy. Lucy is a forty-seven year old African-American, has been openly-gay since she was fifteen, lives in Boston, is an attorney, and is in a relationship in which she is considered the "femme". She and her mate have three children (all boys, ranging in age from 21-27, she birthed all of the children). Her mate is also in her late 40's, and has two children of her own that reside with her ex-husband. These ladies have been in their relationship for 18 years. They were recently "married" here in New York. According to Lucy, they were already married in their hearts.

Now for the answers to my questions, Lucy said she identifies with her feminine side, that she doesn't approve of any woman that "poses" as a man, and she feels that if you're a girl you should act like one. She said she wouldn't ever think about, let alone call her mate by a male title, and she would be appalled by any woman worth her weight in estrogen that allows her kids to call a woman she is in a relationship with "Daddy". She said her children call her mate "Mama" and that she is called "Mom".

Gwen is 23, lives in Virginia, is bi-racial, a college grad that works in retail, is in a new relationship and that she considers herself to be Aggressive or a "stud". She came out when she was sixteen. She stated that she was more in touch with her masculine tendencies, but **KNOWS** she is a woman so she has no need to "pose". She was dating a young lady that had gotten pregnant so that they could have a baby, but; unfortunately the baby was lost to them. She also signed the baby's birth certificate as "Mother number 2" because she didn't want to confuse the child if it had survived. Her new mate is "femme" and the only time she allows her to refer to her in a masculine terminology is during sexual relations.

Gwen's new mate has a child under the age of five and he will not be allowed to call her anything but her name. She is of the opinion that children will be confused if they are allowed to call a woman by a male title, so she is determined to not allow this in her life, as she doesn't approve of this action. She said children deserve to know the differences between a male and a female, and she's offended by her "AG sisters" who don't teach their kids to know these differences.

Now Sonia's answers might be the cause of the nonsense that she deals with on a daily basis. Sonia is a Caucasian thirty-eight year old who came out when she was twenty, lives in New York City, is the "Stud" in her 15 year relationship, has two kids—ages 3 and 7, (both girls) and since becoming a lesbian has been in two relationships with women with kids. She says she used to be Femme, but decided that she liked being viewed as masculine because as a femme, she felt like a wimp. When asked if she approved of AG females "posing" as men, she flew off the handle and took this personally, because she said she wasn't "posing", that she really felt like a man on the inside. All of her mates have been asked to call her "Daddy", and the children of those mates also refer to her as such.

She obviously approves of the children calling her by this masculine title, and in fact; demands that they do so. When asked if she thought that this might confuse the children, she simply shrugged her shoulders and said she thought of herself as a dude and that's how she wanted everyone to view her. Now ladies in the lesbian community, please do not get angry at what I am about to say, but this needs to be addressed now, so that you can begin to better understand what the point of this book is. I wanted to slap the taste out of her mouth! Not because she's gay, but because she condones confusing children.

As a very feminine woman, I am offended that another woman could be so callous as to think that children don't have enough to worry about without being forced to purposely be confused on whether "DADDY" has a vagina or a penis! I have been friends with lesbians, both femme and studs, and I look damned good when I put on my "boyish" clothes. What I learned from my gay friends however is that many lesbians feel that they were meant to "be men".

Now again, I am considered bi-sexual, yet I never felt like a man at any time in my life. Since sexual behavior is a choice (NO-ONE IS BORN KNOWING THAT THEY WOULD LIKE TO HAVE SEX WITH THE SAME SEX OR ANY SEX, for that matter), why would someone force their choices into someone else's life, especially a child? How is that fair to them or anyone in this lady's life? Children deserve a happy home, filled with joy and laughter, love and more than that; RESPECT! If you are a woman in the full physical description of the word, that means you have a vagina. At what point did being a lesbian become about ***NOT*** recognizing this very crucial FACT?

The dictionary says that a "lesbian is a WOMAN who engages in SEXUAL BEHAVIOR WITH OTHER WOMEN". Last time I checked, A WOMAN IS a FEMALE of the human race identified by her VAGINA! She has a menstrual cycle for close to 50 years, which means PMS every month for however long she has a cycle. So forgive me if I sound like I am "judging" but, at what point during PMS do you "feel" like a man? When you are bloated, or maybe during the severe abdominal cramps, or better yet, when you're wiping blood off of your vagina after taking off or taking out your sanitary napkin or tampon?

I have yet to meet the man that has a period. If he exists, I'd love to interview him for my next book. Now ladies, if you are in a relationship with another woman, by all means, PLEASE ENJOY LOVE. If there are children involved, explain that you love this other person like you love them, but this person is not their father because fathers, (be they good ones or bad ones) are MEN, with penis'. And your mate, being a female, does not have a penis so they shouldn't be referred to as any kind of masculine title.

Sisters, if you are one of the "Sonia's" out there, I implore you to please think about the long term consequences of your actions on your children. No mother I know of in history WANTS their child to grow up and be gay, but we accept it because we realize that it's a lifestyle CHOICE. Once the decision has been made by that child that he/she is gay, the only thing we can do is pray that they find true love and are happy. What else can we do? Back to the topic of lesbians who view themselves as "men", girls don't have a penis; but I think you know that already.

How can you insist that you are "a grown ass man" when you aren't behaving like a "grown-up" period? On top of this, you are causing needless drama for yourselves, as well as for your other sisters in the gay community by "posing" as males. How are you doing this, you may ask. Well, the answer is simple. If you so boldly refer to yourself as a lesbian, yet you're still "acting like a man" through your behavior; then you have forgotten what the word lesbian means: a WOMAN that only engages in sexual behavior with other women. How do you condone "acting masculine" to the point of allowing children to be confused about whether or not you are male? Now for my lesbian sisters who are a bit out of sorts with me, you may be saying, "who gave this fat bitch the right to judge us, if I want my kids to call me Daddy; why is this any of her business?"; I have news for you.

I am not now, and never have been a man, and to all extents and purposes; neither have you. So if I sound a little harsh with my comments, that's only because YOUR guilt at YOUR careless behavior has been a problem for YOU from the start. If you treat a child with parents involved in a same sex relationship like they are different from children with parents involved with in a heterosexual relationship, you run the risk of that child becoming confused as to the nature of the physical sex of either parent.

You say you're PROUD to express your love of your partner and that you should have the same basic rights as a hetero-couple yet you are behaving like you are ashamed of your ***gender***. I believe that you have unnecessary drama, not because you're gay, but because you have identity problems. You can't be considered an AG, a stud, a top, a butch or any other title attributed to lesbians with more masculine tendencies, because these masculine titles are attributed to "WOMEN". If you are the "Daddy", then physically; you are a man. Not a rubber-enhanced, poorly constructed version of a male.

I hope I have managed to at least wake you up to reality just a little bit. I could go on for days, explaining why you shouldn't even be gay, but to each his/her own. I sincerely pray that if you consider yourself to be a lesbian, that you embrace your ***gender for your self-worth*** and the added sense of ***gender pride***! I pray that you give this matter of confusing the children with your gender-bending some serious thought. You can't teach our daughters to be proud of their female accomplishments, if you can't even admit that you are a FEMALE!! And you for damned sure can't teach our sons that a woman makes a better father than they can (as males).

You may think that only women suffer with SPDS and that only "weak" females will have drama playing havoc on their daily living; but you are WRONG!! Men, (real men); have more daily drama than women because they aren't only dealing with the drama in their lives, but also; the drama in the lives of their counter parts who seem to breathe for drama. His mom, his aunt, his sister, and pretty much every female that's a part of his life will have some kind of drama. Have some common sense or if not; have some compassion. Men have it hard enough without us making life more difficult for them by having to explain why you aren't their kids' "DADDY".

Oh, and one more thing. STOP putting yourself into a situation where your gender is in question. I used to watch a talk-show that turned into a media circus because of the deceits being purposely perpetrated by guests on other unsuspecting guests. You know which show to which I am referring. The one where GROWN MEN in dresses fighting with REAL WOMEN over their mates, grown women in trousers fooling other women by "posing" as men, etc. All that show did was to explain what I have been discussing through this whole book. Self-Perpetuated Drama Syndrome is the unnecessary act of behaving inappropriately. How in-appropriate is pretending to be the opposite sex? Even better, how in-appropriate is it to try to "trick" an unsuspecting mate with that deception?

If you are in a same-sex relationship, by all means; revel in it. Just don't assume that you can change who you really are. For my so-called "successful post-op, transgender" folks, you still were born a female, and you will never know what a REAL MAN feels. You will also carry the burden and guilt within yourself of removing all the light from your parents eyes as they look at their little "girl" and see how handsome their "big boy" grew up to be. Like most parent-child relationships, the mother feels like she will do just about anything to ensure her daughter grows up to be a "REAL WOMAN", one who is a real "B.I.T.C.H!"

That's "Beautiful, Intelligent, Thoughtful, Caring and, Honest!" I want you lesbian sisters to refer to yourselves as "Mommy" because Mommy is Beautiful to GOD First, herself and her mate, and last but Never LEAST HER KIDS! Daddy is a name for the FATHER OF YOUR KIDS, NOT YOU OR ANOTHER WOMAN!! I capitalized a lot because I can't emphasize this enough. What YOU do today directly affects what your kids and EVERYBODY ELSE'S KIDS that they come in contact with DO TOMORROW!!! Remember that old poem "It takes a village to raise a child"? What you teach in your yard today will be on the schoolyard by 3:00pm the next school day!

I was raised under the roofs of a FEW GOOD WOMEN. I was blessed with two mothers, one who is no longer amidst the living. None of the women that raised me were "perfect", but they were and are PROUD TO BE WOMEN! With all their parenting mistakes, (and there were more than a few, I'm being honest); these WOMEN raised a REAL B.I.T.C.H!! I am certain that you're mom raised you to be yourself as well. Be who you were raised to be—YOURSELF! You feel more comfortable in men's clothes, then; by all means, dress in men's clothes. If you want to be in love with another woman, then I am ecstatic that you found love at all. But know that your kids will show you what you taught them.

If you were really a "DADDY", you will never experience love as a woman. If you deprive yourself the love of "a GOOD WOMAN"(meaning YOU loving yourself); you will never know what that kind of love feels like, because a man can't know what a woman feels like in her Female SOUL. People always try to analyze themselves, but if you suffer with SPDS; you will always come up with your in-adequacies instead of celebrating your achievements. Your children will grow up in a state of constant drama if you do not seek a higher understanding of what's right, wrong, or indifferent. If that's what you seek, then I am sure you will find it.

If you opt to do right by your sons and daughters by being a "GOOD MOTHER" you will find that the children will be well schooled in being whichever gender they are proudly AND appropriately behaved. Let the men be "DADDY" so that if He turns out to be a Dead beat, and your relationship with your mate is not working and you split, you still won't be referred to as the "DEAD-BEAT DADDY". See how simple that is? We've spent more than enough time discussing this topic, let's move on.

CHAPTER 10: WHAT HE REALLY THINKS-HOW MEN ARE AFFECTED BY YOUR DRAMA

It's time for the fire-works. Okay ladies, I am going to the fellas for this chapter because even after everything you've read, I am sure that some of you girls still need a male's input to seal the deal, so to speak. I have quite a few male friends that come from my days as an adult entertainer. (I addressed one aspect of my "part-time profession" in chapter 8, but I am an over-all friendly person, and I like men, a lot). I have always looked into the male-female relationship as a possible case-study for a book. I think it's only fair to see what men think about the topics discussed in this book. You might find their answers to my questions to be useful and insightful.

I have asked ten men, ranging in age from 18-45, a few questions. The questions are linked to each chapter so far. Some of them are "yes/no" type questions, the others required in-depth answers. I was a little surprised to see some of these men really WANTING to answer these questions for me, because I was under the impression that most men don't care about a females DRAMA! I was so very wrong! Not only are they interested, they have some really good advice for you ladies.

Now as you all know, due to the number of pages this book; I was once again forced to choose only three of these men whose answers will be used. To all the others, I thank you and so do the women we are trying to help get "cured" from SPDS. So without further ado, I would like to introduce you to Warren J., Maxwell, and Rich T. (again, not their real names). It was a hard choice to make, but these three fit my needs exactly. I will be making a couple of references to the other guy's answers too. I am sticking with these three because of their ages and backgrounds.

I started with the youngest, Warren J. He is 18 years old, just graduated from high school, still lives at home with his grandmother, (Dad's Mom, because of his mother's living situation) and has only had one romantic relationship with a girl since he started dating last year. He's pretty much your typical teen boy. Healthy, happy, strong and intelligent, just like his parents wanted him to be. Warren's experiences with SPDS are limited to the females in his family.

I asked Warren and the other men in my interviews if they know any women who could be identified as suffering with SPDS, and he immediately answered "my great-grandma and my dad's mom". When asked if he could describe why he thinks they have this drama, he stated plainly that they were women, and it's in a woman's DNA to be embroiled in daily drama. He said that girls are born with the "drama gene", and so they are more prone to have drama, needless or otherwise.

So far, this young man has only had one relationship (romantic), so he wasn't really sure if SPDS caused his break-up with this young lady, but he does feel that she over-reacted to certain situations and had a lot of pent-up anger at life in general. When I asked him if he could offer some advice to his female peers that may save them from suffering with SPDS in the future, he said simply "girls need to not just HEAR words from men, they need to LISTEN to THEMSELVES and learn the difference between a genuine compliment and a come-on line!"

Now, coming from an 18 year old, this is actually good advice. I then asked him to share his thoughts on why he feels his parents suffer with SPDS. He said that his grandmother and great-grandmother are from the school of "older folks who have never had a man show them respect unless they portrayed the "strong woman" persona. When I asked what that was, he said "women throughout history have had to take a stand against being viewed as the weaker sex, and many of them felt that they were only going to succeed in life by taking on what had been viewed as masculine behavior to get the respect they truly deserved".

What kind of masculine behavior? Talking loud, dressing loud, and doing a lot of manly things, like smoking and drinking and working jobs that only men of their time would do: Construction, industrial jobs, etcetera. Now as a mother of semi-adult children, these responses kind of shocked me. I asked did he think that SPDS was hereditary and he immediately responded "Hell yes"! He stated that every woman learned how to be a woman from the women in their family, and if great-grandma suffered with SPDS, it would be safe to theorize that her mom did as well, and so will her daughters, because that's all they knew. Can you say "DEEP"?

Now my next subject is Maxwell. Max is 41, recently divorced, has 2 children that he is raising (the judge gave him full custody of his teenage daughters, ages 13, and 17). When I asked what kind of SPDS he's experienced, he laughed and asked me was I joking? "No, I am serious" was met with "where do I start?" I said to start with the marriage. He didn't finish for an hour, explaining why marriage doesn't work for him. What I heard was a lot of complaints, but overall; he needed to vent. Women need to learn to listen, women need to be more decisive, women need to love themselves more, and women need to remember their PLACE!

Now I really didn't get a chance to ask him all of my questions, because he is bitter, his wounds too deep and the disappointment too fresh. I did, however; notice that he repeated what a woman needs to do a lot. I asked him finally why he feels that a woman "needs to do anything to improve her SPDS", and he responded, "obviously women have drama because they choose too, and to make a man's life miserable". Can we say "living in a glass house and have bricks in hand"?

In order to keep this from turning uglier than it already was, I dared to ask him why he thought his marriage of 27 years failed. Why the hell did I do that? I'll just relay his answers and if you have been paying attention since chapter 1, you'll be able to spot all of the symptoms of SPDS, displayed by his ex and HIMSELF. In order to understand his ending, you'll need to see the relationship from the start.

Maxwell met Danielle while they were still in high school. He was the "cute guy" and she was known as the "nerdy, fat chick". He became her friend, her protector from the "cute, skinny girls, a.k.a., the bullies". As they got older, she slimmed down a little bit, then they began to date. They went to the prom together, and that night Danielle got pregnant. He didn't want to be in a relationship past that summer because he was leaving the state to go into college that fall. He was 19, she was 17 and neither of them wanted to be parents. When her parents told his parents that they would have him arrested for statutory rape if he didn't marry her and make her and the baby legitimate, they got married.

Danielle was already suffering with low self-esteem, and felt like a charity case. Four months into the marriage and pregnancy, she lost the baby. Max tried to have the marriage annulled, but failed because of financial constraints. So they stayed married. Eventually, "playing house" turned into two children, and the hell marriage can become when neither partner is concerned with each other's well-being. Maxwell resented Danielle because he felt that he was "set-up" by her parents. Danielle resented him for allowing her parents to make her look desperate and for not saying "NO" when they demanded the marriage. I noticed that there was a lot of parental involvement, but no mutual communication between the couple.

I also noticed that in the amount of time Maxwell was complaining about their years together, he blamed her for everything. He complained about her in-appropriate behavior when they would venture out doors together, her consistently, in-appropriate attire, her profanity towards him and everyone else, her argumentative behavior when he addressed these habits to her, her finally leaving him for a woman who tried to make his young daughters refer to her as "Daddy", her lack of self-worth. By the time he was through venting, we were both crying for the love that never was.

After the "Kleenex moment", I asked if he ever loved her and his response was so straight to the point that again I was shocked. "How can you love someone that HATES themself so much that they sabotage every bit of their own happiness, so that they can complain about it to someone else that they hate just as much because that person WANTS to love them?" I asked him if he could change one thing about Danielle that might have made her a better wife, what would it be, and he said "I would change how she views herself". Maxwell, I wrote this book just for her and every other woman who suffers with SPDS.

Rich T. requires a little bit of understanding. The women in his life (mother, aunts, four of eight sisters, a niece and his only girlfriend) enacted so much drama in his life that he decided to become a celibate and anti-social male. This is a special case of SPDS coming home to roost, so to speak. Rich is kind of shy around women due to his female family members and all their foolish behaviors. Let's give an overview of his 45 years on this planet.

Rich was born to a set of abusive parents, the only boy in a family of nine children. He is actually the middle kid. According to Rich, His mother was more abusive than his father, who got fed up with constant pregnancies, and left the day before his youngest sister was born. As a boy, his mom felt that all that went wrong in their lives was his dad's fault, and when the father left, she turned to blaming Rich, because there was no other man in the household.

Rich suffered physical, emotional, verbal, financial and sexual abuse at the hands of these women in his life. It came as no surprise then that he thought about becoming a homo-sexual at one time. He never did go through with having sex with another man though. When I asked him what made him change his mind, he said that he couldn't allow the bad things in his life make him someone he is not, and he isn't gay. After telling me his story, I could totally feel his apprehension about getting into a relationship with a woman again.

Rich stated that his mother was abused by her father, and then his father, and just kept up the cycle of abuse with her kids. He says that every time she got beat up or mistreated, he and his younger sisters would catch hell, (meaning she transferred her anger to the defenseless children). When Rich met his ex-girlfriend, his older sisters would fight with her out of jealousy, because the four oldest girls had been making him perform sexually in-appropriate acts on them.

One of his niece's was thought to be his child. A blood test determined that he wasn't the child's father, but the stigma has forever changed his life. His girlfriend left him and he has been single and celibate for over ten years. When I interviewed him, there were times when his story made me ashamed to be a woman, and other times when I was ashamed that his family members were female. I asked him if he felt like these women were victims of SPDS, and he said yes so fast, I didn't hear him respond.

I asked him how he coped with the abuse. He said he realized that his experiences taught him to turn all the negative emotional vibes into art, (he sculpts metal and his work is gorgeous by the way). He's a devout Christian, so he learned to pray more. He understands all too well how abuse becomes an ongoing thing if it's not addressed, then dealt with. He tried to commit suicide over 20 times before he moved out of his mother's house at the age of 19. Then he got accepted to art school, and put his past behind him.

Now Rich's story is his motivation, he turns his past pain into high-priced art. He says every one of his pieces reflects how he dealt with the SPDS of his female family members. I asked him the question about changing one thing about one of the females in his life and his answer is still my favorite. He said, "I would change my mother's low self-esteem, because I know that is the root of her problems. I would pray that GOD shows her that she is worthy of love, that she deserved to have the men in her life love and protect her. But most of all, I would give her the courage to stand up for herself, to want better for her and us".

Now, those who know me, or at least think that they know me, know exactly what I mean when I say, I could punch these so-called "women" in the FACE!! TWICE!! I understand being abused, raped, and just mistreated, but do women think they have "dibb's" on being wronged? Do we think that JUST BECAUSE we're female that it gives us "SOLE OWNERSHIP" to being WRONGED? It would seem so, due to the fact that this mistreatment being turned inward is causing more OUTWARD SPDS than ever before. I am frustrated for everyone who is directly affected by unnecessary drama. I am reaching out to tell you that I have survived so much through GOD's decisions for me. HE, in HIS infinite wisdom, "puts us through hell!" so we can appreciate Heaven more!

Rich T., I know it was hard to disclose so much of your personal experiences with SPDS, and I hope that your mom, aunts, sisters, and every other woman out there appreciate the efforts being made on their behalf to tell the world that we are in total control of our DESTINIES. They need to self-evaluate, see where they can use change in their lives, and try to alleviate the Drama. Just because you were victimized in the past doesn't me you can't be VICTORIOUS in your future!

You just have to want to be a victor, and not continue to be a victim. Every adult over the age of 18 has the power to change any negative situation into a positive solution for their own betterment. Now it's up to you. If you want change for the better to become a fixture in your life, learn and then act on how to do it. You can see change when you open your eyes and HEART to make change!

CHAPTER 11: LIVING WHAT YOU LEARNED

Finally, the last word! I know you have been anxiously awaiting my summary of the last 9 chapters, to see me tie it all together. I am almost done. I now know that I wasn't the only person who needed to know that "being GROWN" takes a lot more work on my self-improvement and mentality. I also now know that this book was written as a helping tool to upgrade the quality of my life. GOD had me write it out, so that I could benefit from writing it as much as you can benefit from reading it.

I covered the majority of topics concerning SPDS, and how we handle the daily, self-inflicted stresses we have gone through. I have touched on things like Age-Appropriate Behavior, Dressing, and Acting so that we can better use our GOD given gifts to have less stress and drama in our lives. I have given time-tested advice on rearing children, getting rid of toxic situations (and people), and raising your self-view. I even touched on a couple of "taboo" subjects: Chapters 8 and 9.

Overall, I think I made my initial point, which is to show that the majority of our problems can be alleviated by simply being comfortable enough in our *"growness"* to recognize that at the root of every problem, is the CHOICE to change it to the Solution, sans drama. I know that I made a few folks uncomfortable with my opinions, and that's exactly what I set out to do. If you are caught in a perpetual state of self-awareness, then you behave with a bit more discernment and discretion making SPDS obsolete. I am just trying to make others realize that they shouldn't get comfortable with living a Drama-filled life, that they should be so UNCOMFORTABLE with the daily drama that they CHOOSE to make POSITIVE CHANGES for themselves.

Now, I can say "I AM GROWN!" Now, I can be sure that MY PERSONAL SPDS doesn't have to keep me ignorant to feeling better about MYSELF! I pray that you allow yourself to feel the same way about yourself. Drama is only for ACTORS!

I love watching it unfold on TV, and in the movies, but in MY life? Not so much anymore. Ladies, your life is your own. Live it to the fullest. Just keep in mind that HOW you live is what makes you WHO YOU ARE!! So with that thought said, I pray for my continued "GROWTH" and yours. No-one should be suffering with SPDS after reading this book, but if you are, my advice is for you to "GROW THE __UP!" YOU fill in the blank!

<u>THE END . . . ?</u>

"CALMING ME DOWN" TEA RECIPE, AND OTHER HELPFUL TOOLS TO HELP "CURE" S.P.D.S.

Orange and Mint Tea: This is a tea that helps calm nerves, as well as makes you feel better during a cold and other feminine ailments (menstrual cramps) and just taste good. I make a container and keep it in my fridge just for drinking purposes.

What you will need: A medium sauce pan

Your favorite mug or teacup

The need to drink tea

Ingredients: One small orange, peeled, save the peelings

Three mint leaves

2 teabags, any flavor

1 quart of boiling water

1 cup of granulated sugar, or half a cup of artificial sweetener

Recipe: In the pot of boiling water, add the tea bag, the mint leaves, and the orange peel. Let boil for 3 minutes. Remove from flame, add sugar and stir until the sugar is dissolved. Cover tightly and let sit until cool. Once this is done, strain the liquid of the peels and leaves and the tea bag. Put into a container and serve warm, or over ice. Either way, it's GOOD!

<u>Now some stores that cater to "Plus Sized Princesses" that carry very nice things in sizes over a size 12.</u>

Shopper's World, Fashion to FIGURE, TORRID, Fredericks of Hollywood, Fashions for Less, and CONWAY'S are some of my favorites. Also, Rainbow Plus and Ashley Stewart. For shoes, Payless Shoe Source, Of COURSE!!

These are just some of the stores I shop in. I am sure you have some to add to the list. Just remember to BUY YOUR SIZE wherever you shop! Happy NEW YOU, Girlfriend!

RECOMMENDED VIDEO GAMES AND OTHER RECREATIONAL ACTIVITIES TO HELP AVOID DRAMA!!!

For you girls who tend more often than not to deal with drama violently, here are some good video games that I play to relieve stress. (They also help me learn people skills, and allow me to commit acts of aggression within the confines of my own home).

The Sims series, The Saints Row Series, 25 To Life, The Grand Theft Auto Series, L.A. Noire, Ultimate Marvel vs. Capcom 3, Brain Age, The Mario Bros. series, and the Sonic series.

Books are a good way to avoid drama AND increase your intellect. Leaving *"ghetto-erotica"* completely out of the picture, here are a few authors that I'd recommend.

The Harry Potter books, (because women LOVE magic.), All of the Clive Cussler (The Dirk Pitt and The NUMA books are my favorite!), James Patterson, and Stephen King Novels, (because women LOVE adventure and a epic battle between good and evil),The Vampire Chronicles by Ann Rice and The Anita Blake Vampire Hunter series by Laurell K. Hamilton, (because every vampire BEFORE The Twilight Series were OLD enough for GROWN WOMEN to enjoy, and They didn't sparkle!). These are my favorite authors and their stories make you want to read more. How does this benefit you? If you're reading, you're NOT embroiled in any DRAMA, except the one unfolding in your book.

Thank You's and Acknoweledgements

<u>Thank You GOD</u>! YOU and YOU ALONE Did This! I PRAISE YOUR HOLY NAME! I thank you for YOUR WILL and I welcome it! THANK YOU!

The following people have been so instrumental in presenting to the public this first step on my final journey. I love BOTH of My Sons, Boy and Ju-Ju, Mommy couldn't complete this without you. Sexy Son kisses are . . . . You know the rest. To my daughters, and daughters-in law, thanks for your input. READ THE WHOLE DAMNED BOOK!!!!! And if you missed something, read it again!! I love you all. Nitty. I don't know where to begin. You are the blessing I prayed for so many moons ago. You've loved me like NO-ONE ELSE ever loved me! God made us for each other. Thank you. I love you. MY Sisters, Sistahs and "Cuzzins"! I love all of your gorgeous behinds!! "Not Nary A'ONE OF US IS UGLY—INSIDE OR OUT!" Charlie, my strength, my SISTER! When I was at my lowest points, you still loved GOD for me, and me for you. I am so HAPPY that you found(*ling) me (smile) and helped me to "belong and be accepted". SISTER/BBW/BFFs 4e! Special Shout to my FB FAM! Tweet me or hit my g-mail!

TO ALL MY HATERS: KEEP UP THE GOOD WORK!! I'm still praying for all of you, anyway!

Now, JW, AO,EM, DW, Lil JW, MW, and any other male who actually HELPED and encouraged me to write this book and take control of my destiny and place it on the alter. Thanks for teaching, guiding and showing me exactly what men want in a woman. You have all influenced my life in many ways for many years. Love Ya, lata! Science, my brother! We did it! And "Margo's Jus' Saying'" is gonna be a hit! Welcome back THE 80"s!!

GMV—the soundtrack to my life will be blended by you and Pooch! Did I miss any body? If so, I'm shouting you now! My hairstyle in the photo on the back jacket cover was created by C. Oldham, the best sister ever! The back jacket photograph was taken by the love of my life. Thanks, Daddy. Karen, Hope, Krista and every one at I-Universe: I am SPEECHLESS! THANK YOU ALL SOOOOOOOO MUCH!! Hugs and Wishes of love to all of you! I hope our future endeavors bring blessings for us all!

Be on the lookout for Book 2 in the "Grow The—UP!" series: GTBU2—BBW's and Hating each other! If you enjoyed book 1, book 2 is going to rock your world! In this second installment of M.J. Norman's advice series, she speaks directly to the PLUS SIZE Princesses about being mean to one another. Ms. Norman addresses the problems that keep BBW's separated from their "sisters" in the "Plus size" community, expelling the myth that all "Fat Girls" are the same! She defines the differences between "A Big Girl" and "A FAT BITCH", and has you laughing with her use of "common knowledge" about the subject.